STUDENT MOVEMENT IN INDIA

Owing to the antiquity and rarity of this book, certain pages are regrettably absent, and readability is compromised due to the blurring of the original text. If you possess any insights regarding the availability of these missing sections, kindly inform us. Your assistance is crucial in ensuring the completion of this significant work for the benefit of future generations.

STUDENT MOVEMENT IN INDIA

PRABODH CHANDRA

GYAN

Published by

Gyan Publishing House
5, Ansari Road
Daryaganj, New Delhi-110002
Phone: 011-47034999, 9811692060
E-mail: books@gyanbooks.com

Distribution Network
gyanbooks.com
India, USA, Canada, UK, Australia

ISBN: 978-93-7014-379-1 (PB)

First Published, 1938

2nd Impression 2025

Printed at: Gyan Press, Delhi.

STUDENT MOVEMENT IN INDIA
Author: PRABODH CHANDRA

STUDENT MOVEMENT
IN INDIA

by

PRABODH CHANDRA, M.A.
President : Punjab Students' Federation
Sole Delegate, All-India Students' Federation
to : World Student Conference, Budapest
and World Youth Conference, New York

1938

PUBLISHED BY

ALL-INDIA STUDENTS' FEDERATION
PUBLICATION DEPOT
POST BOX NO. 177, LAHORE

TO

UNKNOWN MARTYRS WHO SUFFERED
AND DIED FOR THE STUDENT CAUSE
IN MEMORY

CONTENTS

CHAPTER		PAGE
	Preface	VII
I	INTRODUTION	1
II	INDIA AT A GLANCE	5
III	HISTORICAL SURVEY	12
IV	THE CONSTITUTION OF INDIA	20
V	EDUCATION IN INDIA—ANCIENT	27
VI	EDUCATION IN INDIA—MEDIÆVAL AND MODERN	33
VII	SYSTEM OF EDUCATION IN INDIA	39
VIII	ORIGIN OF STUDENT MOVEMENT IN INDIA	46
IX	STUDENT ORGANIZATIONS IN INDIA	51
X	ALL-INDIA STUDENTS' FEDERATION	53
XI	STUDENT MOVEMENT IN THE PUNJAB	58
XII	STUDENT MOVEMENT IN U. P.	77
XIII	STUDENT MOVEMENT IN BENGAL	85
XIV	STUDENT MOVEMENT IN MADRAS	91
XV	STUDENT MOVEMENT IN BOMBAY	96
XVI	STUDENT MOVEMENT IN DELHI	101
XVII	STUDENT MOVEMENT IN OTHER PROVINCES	108
XVIII	STUDENT MOVEMENT IN BURMA	113
XIX	THE EDUCATED UNEMPLOYED IN INDIA	119
XX	STUDENTS AND POLITICS	127

CHAPTER		PAGE
XXI	STUDENT STRIKES IN INDIA	132
XXII	INTERNATIONAL STUDENT MOVEMENT AND INDIA	142
XXIII	TENDENCIES IN THE STUDENT MOVEMENT	148
XXIV	CONCLUSION	154
APPENDIX		
I	CHARTER OF STUDENT-RIGHTS	156
II	OFFICE-BEARERS OF THE ALL-INDIA STUDENTS' FEDERATION	160

PREFACE

A COUPLE of years ago, there was a move for organizing the All-India Students' Federation. I felt a great desire then, to write a systematic account of the student activities at various places in India. Public life, though fascinating, has one great disadvantage. Amidst tumults and turmoils of public activities, one is bereft of any serious intellectual work. So was the case with me. I had been busy, organizing student unions, holding student conferences and participating in student strikes. I had to address public meetings and for that had to go on an All-India tour thrice.

During April, 1938, while in the thick of the Lahore Ayurvedic College strike, I along with forty other friends, was arrested and sent to jail on a charge of rioting and causing grievous hurt (I do not know up till now on whom did we inflict this hurt). This incarceration gave me a little respite and my thoughts flew back to my old designs. Without pen and ink and without any material, I scribbled many chapters of this book in the dingy cells of the Borstal Institute, Lahore. After a fortnight the Ayurvedic College strike terminated and we were let off without any conviction, never knowing whether we justified the epithet of rioters or not. I longed very much, however, that our release should have come a little later, when I had given the finishing touches to the manuscript. But my resentment on this early release abated, when just after my coming out I was afforded ,an opportunity to welcome Mr. James Klugmann, Secretary, World Student Association, on his recent visit to Lahore. He took the trouble of going through my scheme and gave some valuable suggestions which I have incorporated where-ever necessary.

This book is written for the Indian students with a desire that they should muse over their doings, and for the foreign students with an aim to give them an inkling into the doings of their fellow-brethern in India. The book is written without any motive for the propaganda of a particular cult or ideology. It contains facts and opinions as are prevalent and current in India. It may be, I might have become inevitably egotistical and given more prominence to the activities of my domain. I hope, however, that these personal narratives will help the readers to fill up the gaps and provide a back-ground for the study of bare facts.

I must thank the various local libraries which placed at my disposal all the relevant material for the compilation of this book. I am much obliged to Mr. Pran Nath Mehta, Advocate, Lahore who has written the account of the student movement in the Punjab. I owe my unbounded gratitude to Comrade Roshanlal Verma but for whose kind help and devotion, the book would never have seen the light of the day. He did everything to give it a perfection and saw it through the press as well.

Borstal Jail, Lahore: PRABODH CHANDRA
April 7, 1938.

THE AUTHOR

Prabodh Chandra, M.A.
President, Punjab Studens' Federation ; Chairman, 2nd All-India Students' Conference

GENL.-SECY., ALL-INDIA STUDENTS' FEDERATION

Mr. Ansar Harvani, Aligarh

CHAPTER I

INTRODUCTION

NATIONAL MOVEMENT in India is on the threshold of a new era. The Indian National Congress, the most powerful and perhaps the only political organization is governing in seven out of eleven provinces; the province of Sindh has recently come under the virtual control of the 'Congress'. The socialist movement is also making some headway. The students of India, too, are not behind hand in any way. There is a great *stir* among them too. This book deals with the student movements in India. It is the souvenir which the All-India Students' Federation is going to present to the World Student Conference, Budapest (Hungary) and the World Youth Conference, New York (U. S. A.).

People abroad have quite hazy and vague notions about India. It is really an unpleasant surprize that even in this twentieth century, famous for rapid communications, no true news about India are transmitted abroad. If some of them are, they are coloured. It may be due to colour prejudice or the hostility of the British Press, which does not want to lose India, 'the purest and the precious gem in the crown of the British Commonwealth '. An amusing incident is related by one of our countrymen who went to England for higher studies. One day, while he was lecturing in the metropolis on Indian Constitution, a student stood up and said, " Excuse me if I am irrelevant please. Is not India a land of cobras, serpents, reptiles, wizards and sun-strokes?" Our countryman humorously replied, " To be relevant please these are not included in the Indian Constitution as yet." This small incident reflects how hostile propaganda is carried on abroad against India.

The author has made an attempt, by writing this book, to do his little bit to counteract this false propaganda. More concerned with the student movement, and being the sole delegate to the World Student Conference and the World Youth Conference, he has dealt with the Student movement in India, in extenso.

The first few chapters are devoted to the geographical features and history of India. They become necessary for preparing a background in order to understand and appreciate the chapters that follow. The history of any student movement is mostly linked with history of education, system of education, literacy, the educated unemployed, etc. The author has dealt with these important topics, then, very concisely.

The student movement in India, in an organized form is of a recent growth. It has been treated in detail. The author has enumerated various problems which draw the Indian students closer and closer. In order to focus the trend of this movement, he has analysed the various tendencies predominating this movement.

This picture would not be complete without enumerating the relations between the Indian Student movement and the International Student movement. The various appendices would impart a detailed information about the All-India Students' Federation, the only student organization in India under whose banner all the students unite together to know and to protect their rights.

The author feels confident that this publication will evoke, sympathy and co-operation of various international student and allied movements interested in India, which at the present juncture is busy in its campaign for the attainment of complete national freedom. The youth of the world in general and the students in particular must help Indians in this struggle. The author's aim will be completely fulfilled if the students abroad could clearly and rightly understand India's case for freedom.

This book would equally interest the Indian students. Unfortunately the Indian Press and leaders have not devoted adequate attention towards the student movement. Perhaps, they are too busy in other problems. The author had to search in vain the various libraries for collecting facts and statistics on the student movement. In the publication of this book he has taken that arduous task upon himself. It is hoped that this book would meet the long-felt need.

The students in India are subjugated to various handicaps. There is the alien rule, and then the alien system of education. After educational career, there is the wolf of the educated unemployment that stares them in the full face. Then there is repression and suppression by the various University and educational authorities. Every Indian student must try to understand and appreciate all these problems. He should not sit on the hedge and be a mere spectator now. He must be up and doing. If he does not catch all these problems by their forelocks, he would be thrown to the wall. If he does not take his due share in the emancipation of his motherland, he would be dubbed as a traitor by the coming generations.

The author would think that his labours have been amply rewarded, if branches of the All-India Students' Federation are established at various places and all the students stand united under its banner.

CHAPTER II

INDIA AT A GLANCE

THE Indian Empire extends from north to south for a distance of 2,000 miles and from east to west nearly 2,500 miles, its total area being nearly twenty-two times the size of the British Isles. From the north of Kashmir to the south of India is over 2,000 miles and from Baluchistan to Burma is over 2,500 miles. It extends over forty degrees of longitude and thirty degrees of latitude. The length of the coastal line is roughly 5,000 miles. It occupies a very important position in the south of Asia. Standing at the head of the Indian ocean, it can have a free trade with important countries like America, Australia, Japan and Europe.

Physical Regions.—Broadly speaking there can be three distinct physical regions :—

(1) The Himalayan Region, in the north.

(2) The Indo-Gangetic plain.

(3) The Deccan Plateau of the south.

The Himalayas stretch along the Northern Frontier from Afghanistan to Burma, a distance of 1,500 miles with an average width of nearly 200 miles, forming a natural barrier to the north. On the southern slopes of this barrier are forests, steep gorges and hot valleys; in the middle is a great expanse of lofty mountains covered with eternal snow and on the north there are elevated valleys with but little vegetation. The Himalayas are within two mighty rivers Brahmputra on the east and Indus on the west. Mt. Everest the highest (29,141 ft.) peak in the world, is in the Nepal Himalayas. Gowden-Austen, Nanda-Devi and Naga Parbat are the other important peaks.

The Indo-Gangetic plain lies between the Himalayan region on the north and the Deccan in the south. It occupies greater part of Northern India and is more than 2,000 miles long and 200 miles broad. This plain is watered by the rivers Indus, Ganges, Brahmputra and their tributaries. The land drained by these rivers is alluvial and forms a most fertile region in India. It supports two-fifths of the population and contains the largest number of big towns and cities. It is the most populous part of India. It includes the provinces of the Punjab, United Provinces, Bihar and Bengal.

In the South there rises a great three-side plateau called the Deccan. It slopes from west to east from about 5,000 feet in the Western Ghats to about 1,000 feet in the Eastern Ghats, the rivers with the exception of Narbada and Tapti flowing east into the Bay of Bengal. The rivers are for the most part, of little use for irrigation or communication, flowing through deep and narrow gorges. This region is not smooth and flat but a table-land rising from 1,000 to 3,000 feet above the sea level. The provinces and states of the Deccan table-land are the Central Provinces, Berar, Bombay and Madras Presidencies and the States of Hyderabad and Mysore.

Climate and Rainfall.—As the great part of the counrty lies within the tropics, the climate is tropical, high-temperatures being the rule in low-lands, lower temperatures in high-lands. The rainfall to a great extent is determined by the monsoons, which are seasonal winds. The summer monsoons blow across a large expanse of water and collect moisture. These give 90 per cent. of the rainfall to India. The winter monsoons give a little rainfall on the slopes of the Eastern Ghats. There are three seasons in India,—the hot, rainy and the cool. The hot season is from March to June inclusive, the rainy season lasts from July to October inclusive.

Area of India.—The area of India is 1,808,679 miles—more than twenty times that of Britain or equal to the size of Europe without Russia. The British provinces as distinguished from

Indian states, comprise 61% of the area and nearly 77% of the population. About 90% of the Indian population lives in villages and only 10% in towns.

Population.—The population of India is 352,837,778 (one-fifth of the world). Roughly speaking of every 100 persons in British India, 68 are Hindus, 22 Mohammadans, 3 Buddhists, 3 Animists, 1 Sikh, and one Christian. The annual birth and death rate is the highest in India, being 34·3 and 24·9 respectively.

Indian States.—Indian states are under Indian princes who are under British suzerainty. Their area is 712,508 square miles and they number 600 states. Population of Indian states is 81,310,845. These states are not independent powers, as they are guaranteed security from without by the paramount power which also acts for them in relation to foreign powers and other states, and intervenes where the internal peace is seriously threatened. In return for protection both internal and external, they have surrendered their sovereign power to the British Crown. Under the new constitution, Indian states are allowed to join with British India in the Federation, if half the States' population consents. When the Federation is complete the ruling princes will nominate members to the Federal legislature.

Occupations.—The main occupation of the people of India is agriculture. Nearly 90% of the people till land and earn their living by the sweat of their brow. India is not developed so much industrially, although there are ample resources for it. The reasons are political and best known to the dominating race. Historically speaking, we are reminded of the industrial enterprizes of Indians, when they produced fine muslins during the fifteenth and the sixteenth centuries. They were so fine that a thirty yards long cloth with a width of $\frac{3}{4}$ yards could pass through a finger ring. These textiles were called the webs of woven wind. Now, if voice is raised for the industrial development, we are hushed by the advice that India is not rich in mineral resources; that India cannot compete with foreign industries. Of late there has been some development of the sugar and paper industries. Some protective tariffs have been levied to encourage them. But now they are being withdrawn without any cogent reasons. There are apprehensions that these industries are likely to fail, in face of these handicaps and the special treatment meted out to the British imports. Some villagers are following the occupation of grazing, felling timber and carrying on indeginous industries. The All-India Village Industries Association and the All-India Spinners' Association under the guidance of Gandhiji are striving their utmost to revive the village industries and to make villages self-sufficient. This is yet an experiment of the Gandhian principles to check the growing unemployment and spirit of competition. The following is the trade of India :—

Exports.—Wheat, cotton, tea, rice, jute, oil-seeds, hides and skins, gunny-bags, exported to United Kingdoms, Australia, Austria, Belgium, Canada, France, Germany, Japan, Italy, Norway, Sweden, South Africa and United States of America.

Imports.—The imports from these countries, especially, the United Kingdom, Germany and United States are :—

Cotton piece-goods, machinery, mill-work, iron and steel, railway engines, hardware, chemicals and drugs, motor vehicles, rubber tyres, and tubes, cigarettes, silk-goods, condensed milk, iron, coal, coke, aluminium and tobacco.

The balance of trade always has been in favour of the exporting countries. Among the big cities of India are Calcutta (population 1,419,321), Bombay (population 1,157,851), Madras (population 647,228), Delhi (population 447,442) and Lahore (population 428,747). Under the new constitution all India becomes federated in common central government consisting of Governors' Provinces, the Chief Commissioners' Provinces and those of Indian States which accede to it. Two new provinces have been created : (1) Sindh is separated from Bombay and (2) Orissa is separated from the province of Behar and Orissa. The Act also creates a Federal Court for all India consisting of a Chief Justice of India and such number of other judges as may be necessary. This New Constitution will be dealt in detail in a separate chapter.

CHAPTER III

HISTORICAL SURVEY

INDIA is perhaps the most ancient country where the human civilization flourished earliest. This statement is amply borne out by the excavations at Mohenjodaru and Taxila, the two ancient Indian cities believed to be five or six thousand years old. The perfect buildings, the drainage system and the pottery discovered from these ruins give us an insight into India's ancient heritage.

The ancient history of India is associated with various religious movements which were innovated either by reformers like the Buddha, Mahavir Vardhman, or invaders of the Yeuchi, Kushan and the Hun dynasties. The famous among the Buddhist Kings were : Chandra Gupta Maurya, Asoka, Kanishka and Harsha ; while Samudra Gupta and Chandra Gupta Vikrmaditya were the later Hindu Kings under whose sway there was revival of Hinduism. This period is remembered as the golden period of the Hindu age, when there was spread of education, increase in Sanskrit literature, an all-round contentment among people. Notions about life were permeated with spiritual sentiments. India then, had colonies as far as Java and Sumatra. It had a very prosperous trade and intercourse with Rome and Greece.

The 8th century A.D. brings us to the Mediæval era of the Indian History. Prophet Muhammad spread the teachings of oneness of God and brotherhood of mankind. He had to fight against heavy odds before he could convert the ferocious Beduins of Arabia to his new religion of Islam. India too was not immune from the effects of this new movement. Mahmud Ghaznavi and Muhammad Ghauri were among the pioneer Muslim rulers who invaded India many a time and defeated the various Hindu dynasties which were like a house divided against itself.

The period of the Afghan rule (*viz.*, 1206 to 1526), has been quite uneventful except that there was spread of Islam, and consolidation of small ruling authorities in the imperial Muslim power at Delhi. There were spasmodic attacks by the Mongols of Central Asia. The only outstanding ruler of this period was Alla-ud-Din Khilji who extended his empire to Dawarsamudra a place to the extreme south of India. Hitherto the histories of the North and the South were quite distinct and separate. The Dandkarna forest in central India impeded every kind of communication and intercourse. Mention may also be made of Feroz Tughlak who after his cousin

Muhammad Tughlak—the wisest fool of Indian history—was the first ruler to do something constructive for his subjects. He established a Public Works Department. He took some interest in education too. The insolent behaviour of Ibrahim Lodhi gave a death blow to the Delhi Sultanate ; and in 1526 steps in Babar the pioneer Mughal ruler, on the Indian arena. The Mughal rule extended from 1526 to 1706. Akbar, the great, was the first Mughal ruler who could consolidate the lost kingdom of his father Humayun. Indian history had been mostly chequered with religious conflicts such as imposition of *jazia* and other atrocities. As a far-sighted and sagacious politician Akabar saw the futility of an aggressive religious course. He cultivated cordial relations with the Hindus and the warrior race of the Rajputs. It was in fact, Akbar who could devote some attention for the development of various governmental institutions. It is from his time that we have an insight into the working of an imperial power in its various activities. He established systems of the executive and judiciary. Above all, he evolved a land revenue system to give a fiscal stability to his rule and to further extend the benificent departments.

The Taj at Agra, Red Fort at Delhi and the Shalamar gardens at Lahore are reminiscent of the Mughal love for architecture. Aurangzeb the last important Mughal ruler was possessed of indomitable will. His intense love for his religion developed in him a sense of exclusiveness and puritanism. So much so, that he developed a strong religious prejudice against other communities like the Hindus, the Mahrattas and the Rajputs. His long wars against Bijapur and Golkonda in the Deccan cost him the Mughal empire.

For a time we do not find any imperial power in India. The Mahrattas founded their confedracy in the Maharashtra. There arose two independent states of Hyderabad and Mysore in the Deccan. The Sikhs were emerging out as a great power in the Punjab.

The year 1744 ushers us into the British period. In the sixteenth century the English and the French, eager for discovering new colonies for the expansion of trade, came to India as traders. Soon they found out that it was quite easy to exploit the various Indian rulers and attain a political supremacy. But the two nationalities—the English and the French could not go hand in hand for long. In the Carnatic Wars the English defeated the French after three successive wars. So a trading company (the East India Company) assumed political power. By the Regulating Act of 1773 the British Parliament took over the control of the East India Company. Lord Wellesley under the subsidiary system annexed many Southern States to the British territory. He adopted all means to undermine the Mahratta and Mysore powers. During the regime of Lord Hardinge attention was diverted towards the Punjab ; and after him Lord Dalhousie not only did annex the Punjab, but he got over Oudh, Jhansi, Satara, Camorin and many other states under the doctrine of lapse or under the pretext of inefficient rule. The territorial acquisition after the reign of Lord Dalhousie was thrown to the back ground. The British diplomacy now worked in various social, economic and educational channels. The system of education was westernized. Railways, motor cars and other rapid means of communication replaced the slow-moving vehicles. The various religious and secular evil customs prevalent in the society were abolished by law.

The year 1858 witnessed the Sepoy Mutiny —the first consorted action by the downtrodden Indians against the British Imperial power. The policy of rapid annexation by Lord Dalhousie, the so-called onslaughts on religious and social customs and above all the desire to free themselves from the shackles of the British rule, led the Indians to this mutiny. Though the mutiny took a heavy toll of lives from both the English and Indian sides, yet timely help by the ferocious and valorous Sikhs from the Punjab won the English a great victory. As a result of this mutiny the East India Company was abolished. The sovereignty was assumed by Queen

ONE OF THE FOUNDERS OF
THE STUDENT MOVEMENT IN THE PUNJAB

Pran Nath Mehta, B.A., LL.B., Advocate

PROMINENT STUDENT WORKERS

Seth Make h Chandra

Mulkh Raj Aggarwal

Victoria who acquired the title of the Queen Empress of India.

Lord Lytton (1878) wanted to crush all sorts of Indian aspirations. He passed a Vernacular Press Act (well-known as the Gagging Act) by which he suppressed the freedom of the press. Credit goes to his successor Lord Ripon who not only repealed the Gagging Act but brought into existence many local bodies (Municipal Committees and District Boards) also. Under these bodies he wanted to give the Indians a training in the art of self-government and thus to prepare them for assuming the full political control of India, as promised in the famous Queen Victoria's Declaration of 1858. It was during his time that Mr. Hume, an enlightened Englishman, founded the Indian National Congress, the greatest and the most important political organization in India.

Lord Curzon in 1901 wanted to stem the tide of growing conciousness. During his time a move was afoot to re-organize the system of education on national basis. Lord Curzon was opposed to it. Ignoring Indian opinion, he appointed a University Commission which consisted of all official members. The Bengalees, as a protest against this commission, brought into existence the National Board of Education. In 1906 Lord Curzon brought about the partition of Bengal. This was perhaps his greatest blunder.

A momentous agitation was launched against this partition. It was for the first time that the words Swadeshi and Non-coperation were added to our national vocabulary. Lord Minto subsequently rectified the blunder and repealed this partition.

Signs of consciousness were visible among the Indians who had remained dormant so far. There were two schools of thoughts—constitutionalists and radicals. To the former school belonged Dada Bhai Noroaji, G. K. Gokhale, Madan Mohan Malaviya and to the latter B. G. Tilak, B. C. Pal and Lajpatrai.

The latter began to dominate the Indian National Congress.

In 1914 was the outbreak of the Great War. Indian nationalists of the calibre of Mahatma Gandhi issued appeals to the nation to help the British in this ordeal, believing in reciprocity. And there were big alluring statements issued by the Britishers. Various promises for the constitutional advancement were given. But in the wake of the Great War there came a strict enforcement of the Rowlatt Act, an autocratic measure passed to cope with any emergency during the Great War. Various national leaders were put behind the bars. This led to the first Gandhian Non-cooperation movement of 1921-22. It was based upon truth and non-violence. The movement closed with the introduction of

Montford reforms which introduced dyarchy in the provincial administration.

The dynamic personality of Pandit Jawaharlal Nehru, the growing consciousness among the people, the appreciation of the international problems during the recent years, changed the objective of the 'Congress' from Dominion Status to Complete Independence. The British diplomacy followed dilatory tactics. After three Round Table Conferences the Government of India Act was passed in 1935. This Act comtemplates to establish a Federal Government in India; it has given some autonomy to the provinces. At the same time the Act confers unlimited powers (of veto, certification and ordinance-making) for the 'peace, tranquility and the good government', for protection of the interests of the minorities and some other special powers on the governor. There is a strong opposition to the Federation from all quarters.

CHAPTER IV

THE CONSTITUTION OF INDIA

THE impulse which drove the British to India was not conquest but trade. The Government of India represents the slow evolution from conditions established to meet trading requirements. On September 24, 1599, a few years before the death of Queen Elizabeth and Akbar, the merchants of London formed an association for the purpose of establishing direct trade with the East and were granted a charter of incorporation. The government of this company in England was vested in Governor with a court of Directors.

The collapse of government in India, consequent on the decay of Mughal power and the intrigues of the French gave the officers of the company an excuse to assume territorial responsibility. The Parliament under the Regulating Act, of 1773, appointed a Governor-General and four councillors to administer Bengal, and supremacy of that presidency over Madras and Bombay was for the first time established. Pitts' India Act, of 1784, which established the Board of Control in England, vested the administration of each of the three presidencies in a Governor and three Councillors. Under the Charter Act of 1833, the Company was compelled to close its commercial business and it became purely a political and administrative body holding its territories in trust for the Crown. The same Act vested the direction of the entire civil and military administration and sole power of legislation in the Governor-General-in-Council.

The year 1858 witnessed the Indian Mutiny. The people of India and the various ruling princes made a joint and organized effort to liberate themselves from the clutches of the British rule. The introduction of the alien system of education, the ruthless and indiscriminate annexation of various territories by Lord Dalhousie, the attack on certain social and religious susceptibilities were among other causes for this mutiny. The British Parliament did recognize the force of the Indian sentiments. The East India Company was abolished and by the Act for the better Government of India of 1858, the entire Indian Government was transferred to the British Crown and the entire control passed to the Secretary of State for India acting in concert in certain cases, with a council, which was an advising body. The Governor General was to represent the crown. This Act was followed by the Queen's Proclamation which said: We hold ourselves bound to the natives of Indian territories by the same obligation of duty which binds us to all our other subjects, and these obligations by the blessing of Almighty God we shall faithfully and conscientiously fulfil.

The Indians were not given any representation in any governmental institutions. Even the legislative function was vested in the Governor-General and his Council. The Indian Councils Act of 1892 introduced the principle of indirect election to the legislative councils brought into existence by this measure. This Act gave these legislatures an opportunity of criticism and enquiry, the right of asking questions, the right to discuss the annual financial statement. There was no germ of responsibility introduced by this Act. Indirect election to the provincial and central legislative Councils was based on nomination on the recommendation of various bodies. Few opportunities were provided to initiate any legislation by these members. As a result of strong agitation against the partition of Bengal, and of a growing demand for popular government, was passed the Council of India Act 1909 better known as the Minto-Morley Reforms. By this, the size of the legislatures was further widened. Non-official majority was introduced while indirect representation was adhered to.

Members were both elected and nominated. Elective principle was adopted with restrictions. Certain subjects were reserved for Central Legislature. Restrictions on discussion of the financial statement were relaxed and full discussion on matters of public interest were allowed. Resolutions upon matters of general public importance might also be proposed and discussed. This reform had nothing to do with the introduction of Responsible Government. This Act introduced the principle of communal representation, which was based on the sinister move of divide-and-rule. In order to satisfy the expectations of the Indians after the Great War, was made the famous declaration of August 20, 1917, which laid : The policy of His Majesty's Government, with which the Government of India are in complete accord is that of increasing association of Indians in every branch of administration and a gradual development of self-governing institutions with a *view to progressive realization of responsible government in India,* as an integral part of the British Empire. The Montague-Chelmsford Report resulted in the Government of India Act, of 1919. The Act introduced diarchical form of Government in the provinces. One part of the Provincial Government consisted of Governor and his Executive Council. All the 'reserved subjects' were dealt with by the members of the Executive Council, not responsible to the Provincial Legislature. The other part of the Provincial Government comprised the Governor acting with the ministers, who were nominated by him. A non-official majority was created in the Central Legislature which was vested with same restricted powers of legislation. The Governor-General could exercise the powers of veto, certification and passing ordinances, etc.

The Indian National Congress carried on a strong and vigorous propaganda for the fulfilment of the declaration of August 17, 1920. The 'Congress' wanted Dominion status for India. This demand was not acceded to. The Congress now launched on the Civil Disobedience campaign and changed its goal to Complete Independence. The Parliament sent various Commissions to India, it held three Round Table Conferences, took into considerarion the proceedings of the Indian National Congress, the Muslim League and the All-Parties Conference.

Under the New Constitution India is federated in common central government consisting of Governors' Provinces, the Chief Commissioners' Provinces and those of Indian States who accede to it. Permission is made to Indian Princes to consent to the Federation. If half of the States population consents, the Federation will be proclaimed. The Federal Parliament is to consist of two houses, the lower one to be elected every five years. This lower house of the Federal Assembly, will consist of 250 representatives of British India chosen by Provincial Legislatures (indirect election) and 125 representatives of

Indian States. The upper house called the Council of State is to consist of 150 representatives of British India elected on a special franchise by 100,000 electors. The upper house will be permanent, one-third of its members retiring every third year. There will be Council of Ministers responsible to the Federal Legislature to aid and advise the Governor-General in exercise of his powers except in so far as he is required to exercise in his discretion.

The Provinces will be governed by the Governor with a Council of Ministers to aid and advise the Governor. In some provinces there will be provincial legislatures consisting of two chambers. In other Provinces (Punjab, N.-W. F. P., Sindh, Orissa and C. P.) there will be one chamber. All the members to these chambers will be elected and the majority party in these bodies will form the ministry, which will be responsible jointly and collectively. The provinces will be autonomous, in the sense that they shall be free and independent to legislate upon the provincial subjects. But there are clogs of the governor's special and discretionary responsibilities, his powers of veto, certification and ordinance-making and suspending the constitution in cases of emergency.

A separate Federal Railway authority is established for the regulation, construction, maintenance and operation of Railways. The Act also creates a Federal Court for all India consisting of a Chief Justice of India and such number of other Judges as may be necessary.

The most important features of the New Constitution in India are : Federation of India, Provincial Autonomy, Responsible Government, safeguards and separation of Burma. The Provincial Autonomy is being worked in all the provinces. The Federation is yet to come. There is a strong agitation for breaking it. All the political organizations are unanimous on this issue. The main objections to this are : that election to the Federal Assembly is indirect, nearly eighty per cent of the central expenditure is non-votable, military and foreign affairs are the exclusive concern of the Viceroy, Indian Princes are to nominate 125 members to the Federal Legislature without consulting the state subjects.

One redeeming feature of the New Constitution is that the electorate in the Governors' Provinces is increased from 3% to 14% of the population and 27% of the adult population. About 36 million are enfranchised.

CHAPTER V

EDUCATION IN INDIA—ANCIENT

DURING the pre-historic period the aborigines in India used to live in caves and later on trees. They were brought up by and in nature. So they talked and sang in praise of green woods, gurgling springs, running brooks, wind, rain, and other natural gifts. They had such a fascination and devotion for these natural phenomena, that they felt a kind of spiritual elation. Their reasoning faculty not having developed so much, they invented legends and sang folklores in their praise. It appears there was no system of writing in vogue then for expression. These legends and folkfore descended from generation to generation. This was the first kind of education received by the ancient Indian inhabitants.

There arose a class of literature afterwards, called the *Srutis**, the books the contents of which were communicated by God. The four Vedas—the Rigveda, Atharwa Veda, Samveda and Yajurveda belong to this category. Later on at the advent of the Aryans some sort of writing

---

*The word *Sruti* is derived from the Sanskrit word *Srut* meaning to hear.

came in vogue. Commentaries and explanatory books like the *Brahman Granths*, *Sutras* and *Upanishdas* came to supplement the Vedas. All this literature dealt with religion and spirituality. Some of these books contain inconsistent and allegorical accounts.

Then there were the *Smritis*, meaning remembered (from father to son). They dealt with secular objects. Well-known among these are the *Smritis* of Manu and Yajnivalka. The former advocated and brought into existence the caste system.

During early period the Aryans of different clans used to live in different groups. Worship was regarded as part and parcel of their lives. So with religion was connected the ancient education. Almost every individual was imparted a knowledge of three R's. There was no particular system of education then.

During the later period of the Indo-Aryans, there came the division of caste-system. The Brahmans, the priestly class, were entrusted with the work of education and worship. No definite knowledge of the system of education of that period can be gathered. However, it can be conclusively drawn out by inferences to the Rig Veda, Ramayana and Mahabharata. Sanskrit was the script and language evolved for writing and expression. Grammatically it was fully and scientifically developed; the whole of the literature of that time was written in this language.

The priests who were the preceptors, were held in high esteem. They were respected even by the kings. They held their classes in the open. They were not only responsible for imparting rudimentary knowledge, but in a way had full control over the spiritual life of students also. A student during *Brahmcharya* (earlier part of life) would go out to the hermitage of the priest. There he would lead a life of penance. He had to serve his *Guru* (preceptor) and look to his comforts. As remuneration for education, he would beg alms for him from the neighbouring villages. The priest in return would teach scriptures, deliver sermons and make his disciple quite competent for the struggle of life. He would also teach the use of arms, weapons and missiles for defence and offence. Every young man rich or poor had to follow this course.

As for the females, they were taught and accomplished at home. They would move in society. There was no *purdah*. They could choose a spouse of their own choice in a *Swyambara*. All this goes to prove that female-education, then, received due consideration.

During the later period in about 300 B.C. when the caste system degenerated, the lower classes of Vaisyas and Sudras were debarred from receiving education.

Buddhism was a reaction and reformation of Hinduism. During this period the Brahmans and Kashatriyas (the priestly and warrior classes) completely disintegrated themselves from the Vaisyas and Sudras (the mercantile and the servant class). The latter were debarred from studying Sanskrit scriptures. So they invented Pali (a simplified and colloquial form of Sanskrit). All the Buddhistic literature is written in this language. It is evident that because of conflict between Hinduism and Buddhism education must have been affected to some extent. The Buddhistic monks received higher education in the *Sanghas* (the Buddhistic monastries). Asoka did much for the spread of Pali and Prakrit; while the Guptas later, revived Sanskrit. This revival of Sanskrit was for counteracting the influence of Buddhism. The eighteen *Puranas* were written during this period. They contain fables with some moral interpretation to impress upon the folk the superiority of Hinduism over Buddhism.

It was between the fourth and the seventh century A.D. that some educational institutions were first established in India. There were the famous Universities of Nalanda in Eastern India and Takshshila (Taxila) in Northern India. As many as 10,000 students from India, China, Herat and other foreign countries came to study there. One is impressed to see their excavated ruins even to-day.

During ancient times there was only the spiritual literature. Then the reasoning and analytical faculties developed. It was during the Gupta period that attention was diverted towards other literary topics. The writers began to depict humanity. Kalidasa, the Indian Shakespeare, wrote dramas depicting beauty and ecstacies of human heart. His imagination is unfathomable. His dramas *Shakuntla*, *Meghduta*, *Vikrmorvashi* are read with greatest interest and delight even to-day. Charak and Sushrit the famous medical-men wrote books on medicine. Panini the famous Sanskrit scholar regulated the rules of Sanskrit Grammar. Amar Singh compiled *Amar Kosh*, the Sanskrit Dictionary. The inavsion of Alexander also influenced Indian literature. People wrote books on Arithmetic, Geometry and Astronomy.

The governmental institutions during this period were not so much developed. Moreover, the kings were absolute monarchs. The authority being concentrated in one person, he could not pay adequate attention to education. Still the kings took due interest in it. This increase of interest in literature is amply borne out from the reign of Chandra Gupta Vikrmaditya who kept *nau ratans* (nine gems) at his Court. They included Kalidasa, Amar Singh, Panini and Charak, the well-known scholars of those times.

In short education in ancient India had a spiritual antithesis. It was based upon the principle of equipping every one with the rudimentary knowledge. The educational institutions were, generally, not under the State control. They were run on public charity and donations. There was no particular system evolved or fixed gradations in schools or *Ashrams*. The subjects taught covered a vast range including religion, sociology, economics, astronomy and military science. Generally the schools were open-air ; but subsequently there arose the big residential Universities of Nalanda and Takshshila.

CHAPTER VI

EDUCATION IN INDIA—MEDIÆVAL AND MODERN

DURING the early period of Muhammadan rule Persian literature came to India. There were no regular educational institutions, even then. The mosques and temples were the places of worship and education. Though the dominating class were the Muhammadans, they did not take so much interest in the spread and development of Persian. Mahmud Ghaznavi was the first Muslim ruler who showed literary inclinations and patronized poets like Firdausi. Some of the Muhammadans learnt Sanskrit and Hindi. Amir Khusro and Raskhan wrote both Hindi and Persian literature.

It was not before the time of Feroz Tughlak that any serious attempt was made to develop education. The Urdu language came in vogue during his reign. He built many mosques and employed Ulemas to teach students. He organized some educational institutions even. After him arose what is famously known as the Bhakti school. Though it did not look much after education, yet it evolved a literature which blended religious toleration. To this age belong Kabir, Nanak, Chaitanya and Ramdas. Akbar kept scholars like Abdul Fazl, Faizi, Todar Mal and Bir Bal. Even he could not do much for the spread of education.

Then the education during the next two centuries was altogether neglected. It must not be concluded that there was no progress in literature. Books written during that period covered various topics.

In the early days of its domination in India the East India Company had little inclination for the doubtful experiment of introducing Western learning in India. Lord Warren Hasting's policy was to enable ancient learning develop under the protection of government. In 1813 a sum of a lakh of rupees was set apart for the introduction and promotion of Sanskrit and Persian languages.

The impetus to the introduction of Western learning was the devotion of Christian missionaries. During the reign of Lord William Bentinck was taken the momentous decision of introducing Western Education in India. His council was divided on the advisibility of such a course. Lord Macaulay in his minutes strongly advocated the introduction of English on political grounds. He wanted to westernize Indians in every sphere of life in order to make them forget their ancient culture, literature and mode of living. Moreover such a system could provide cheap clerks for the East India Company. In 1837 English was substituted for Persian as a language for courts. In 1844 Lord Hardinge declared that Government services would be given only to those who received Western education. In the following decade under this Government's patronage Western education took firm root in India, though some Hindus and Muhammadans stood aloof. Sir Syed Ahmad and Raja Ram Mohan Roy did a lot for the spread of Oriental and English education among the two communities in India.

The foundation of University Education was laid in this country with the establishment of the University of Calcutta, Bombay and Madras in 1857. It was followed by the establishment of two more Universities, the Panjab University was founded in 1882 and the Allahabad University followed in 1887. The land-mark in the history of Indian Universities was the appointment by Lord Curzon of a University Commission in the year 1902. The recommendations of the commission were mainly in the direction of reforms in the constitution of Universities. Though the bulk of teaching continued to be in the affiliated colleges, a certain amount of higher instruction now began to be concentrated under the University management. All the Universities were started under official auspices, but a new departure was made in 1916 and 1920. Two new Universities were estabished to serve the special needs of the

Hindus and Muhammadans, founded largely on the efforts of the two communities. The Benares Hindu University came into existence in 1916 and Aligarh Muslim University in 1920. The provisions of faculties of Oriental learning and religious instruction is a special feature of these institutions. Several new Universities are now established all over India.

The types of Universities in India are: (a) *Affiliating University, i.e.*, a University which recognizes external colleges offering instruction in its course of studies; (b) *Teaching University* is one in which some or all of the teaching is controlled and conducted by teachers appointed by the University; and (c) a *Unitary University* is one usually localized in a single centre, in which the whole of the teaching is conducted by teachers appointed by or under the control of the University.

The following are the interesting statistics about education in India.

Students

Year	In recognized institutions	In all institutions (Recognized and Un-recognized)
1930-31	12,056,837	12,689,086
1931-32	12,122,466	12,766,537
1932-33	12,192,137	12,853,532
1933-34	12,491,796	13,172,890
1934-35	12,820,760	13,506,869

Year	Public Fund	Total
	Rs.	Rs.
1930-31	1,79,926,248	2,83,161,401
1931-32	1,68,419,016	2,71,856,622
1932-33	1,54,256,219	2,57,875,868
1933-34	1,56,636,461	2,61,765,186
1934-35	1,57,465,078	2,65,211,420

Professional and Technical Education

Types of Institutions	1935	
	Institutions	Students
Colleges—		
Training	23	1,701
Law	13	7,256
Medical	10	5,028
Engineering ...	7	2,074
Agricultural ...	6	808
Commercial ...	6	2,605
Forest	1	42
Veterinary	4	379
Total	70	19,893

	1933	1934
Total No. of students ...	2,606,470	2,755,051
Total expenditure Rs. ...	3,52,41,216	3,63,59,399

Literacy in the sense of ability to read and write has grown appreciably in the past fifty years, although it is very low as compared with countries in the West. Ninety-five out of 1,000 of the population are now literate. Literacy is much more prevalent in towns than in the country. An analysis of the population of cities shows that 348 out of 1,000 males and only 149 out of 1,000 females are literate, while the corresponding figures in English towns are: 773 males and 434 females. The following tables give the ratio of literacy to population for three years.

Province	Percentage of Literacy		
	1932	1933	1934
Madras	6·2	6·2	6·5
Bombay	6·11	6·11	6·3
Bengal	5·55	5·71	5·92
U. P.	3·13	3·17	3·2
Punjab	5·61	5·50	5·43
C. P.	2·96	3·02	3·11
Assam	4·32	4·3	4·4
Other Areas	...	9·2	9·4

The cost of education per pupil in British ranges from Rs. 15 to Rs. 20 per annum.

CHAPTER VII

SYSTEM OF EDUCATION IN INDIA

THE present system of education prevalent in India is not based on the idea of educing out all that is necessary for the welfare of a citizen. It was founded on the grounds of political necessity as is evidenced by the minutes of Lord Macaulay who in 1835, with all vehemence advocated the introduction of this Western system of education in India. The East India Company needed cheap clerks; it wanted Indians to forget their ancient culture and never get an inspiration of independent thinking from that. So from its very foundation the present system of education cannot stand any intelligent and searching scrutiny. Times have changed; but we find the same old system of the past going on strong.

Education.—There are various kinds of institutions which impart education. They are founded on religious considerations, numerical strength, rural and urban location. But the system of education prevalent in every institution is practically the same. There are three important gradations:

Primary.—This extends to four years. During this period the infant picks up the rudiments of Vernaculars, Mathematics, and Natural Science. Unfortunately there are no nursery and kindergarten schools. All the students are often huddled up in one room and there is only teacher to teach them.

Secondary.—This extends to six years, during which students pick up English, Mathematics, General Knowledge, Vernacular and Classical languages. In short, all the subjects are jumbled up together. They are taught in such a short time and in such a hopeless manner that no impression is created upon the mind of the students and no interest is created for any particular subject.

College-Education.—The college education continues for four years to entitle a student to secure a degree. Even here every student has to study four or five subjects.

Yet strangely enough, even after this education for fourteen years, students are practically misfits in society. They cannot be called educated in the true sense of the word. They have no knowledge of literature or of natural science. These gradations in no way equip the students for their struggle in life.

The curriculum is not based on any reason or sense. The various subjects are jumbled up together. Every student must study them all. They do not create any interest; nor are they in any way helpful in life. Just imagine a student studying Sanskirt, Mathematics, Geography and English together.

This system of education is breeding too much unemployment. During the times of Lord Macaulay this system might have provided clerks for the government but in 1938 even these posts are denied to the educated. All the government and local departments are full to their saturation.

Unlike other countries no vocational education is imparted to the students. There is a long-felt necessity for opening technical, vocational, veterinary, agricultural, industrial, arts, engineering, mining, weaving and other such like institutions. But the government of the day is either quite indifferent or raises the plea of paucity of funds, although more than 2/3 of the central budget is spent upon the military and the defence of the country; and this is a sheer fraud on the tax-payer, who has to go without any useful education.

System of Examinations.—The system of examinations is quite hopeless. It is not based on 'units' or 'terms' as in the foreign Universities. The examinations must take place only once a year and on a fixed day. The success or failure of a student is focussed on that particular moment. How much diligently he might have worked throughout the year, yet if he cannot do well on that day, he is doomed. The matter does not end there. Any student may get through in all subjects, yet he is declared 'fail'. There is an overriding provision for the aggregate, unheard of anywhere. Furthermore, if a student fails in one subject once, he has to take the whole examination again! Thus the poor Indian student is always in the quagmire of examinations.

Teachers.—The greatest defect of the system lies in the teaching staff. There are no good training colleges to impart training to the teachers. Mostly persons who have been a complete failure in their educational career, become the custodians of the morality and the welfare of the young students. It is really a sight to see them using the schoolmaster's rod when they themselves are helpless to teach anything. Teaching profession is the last resort of any Indian. The reasons are not far to seek. In the first instance, educational institutions are mostly under the direct or indirect control of the government. So no national aspiration can provoke any one to become a school-teacher.

Secondly, teachers in India are mostly ill-paid. Most of them do not get more than £1 a month. This hardly makes both ends meet. But foreign imported teachers are paid very fat salaries. They are mostly persons from the British Universities. The other day the Panjab University has decided to appoint a permanent paid Vice-Chancellor. He is not to be an Indian.

Female Education.—Indians though conservative, have of late recognized the importance of female education. Now they recognize that women are as much destined to play their part in the building up of nation as men. In the case of female wrong laid education, too, the government has not made any adequate provisions. There are only a few female schools, while higher female education is altogther ignored. For instance, there is only one government college for women in the Punjab.

The subjects included in the curriculum are not to the taste of females. Even a layman would recognize that a woman must be taught household and domestic subjects like cookery, sewing, domestic economy, household accounts, art, painting and music. But the females have to swallow a bitter pill. Instead they have to study Mathematics, Persion, Sanskrit and Biology, etc.

Educational Institutions.—A criticism of the system of education will not be complete without making a reference to various educational institutions. As already mentioned the various institutions are run either by the government, and local bodies or by private individuals. The last class of these institutions call for a special attention. These denominational institutions attract the largest number of students, because they provide education at a very low cost. These denominational institutions have played a great part in the national struggle. They allow students freedom of speech and discussion, which is denied in government institutions. Many of our leaders sprang from these institutions. Many of these denominational schools and colleges have suffered a lot during various movements.

Though all the schools and colleges are subjected to the same old system, yet revolt is visible against this. Dr. Rabindra Nath Tagore's Santinekatan, Jamia Millia Islamia, Delhi and Gurukul Kangri are its instances. These institutions have got their different gradations. In Dr. Tagore's Santineketan there is open-air education. There is no fear of school master's rod. Examinations are conducted on more humane lines. Sirineketan (Agricultural Institute) there, imparts education for the rural uplift. Will not the reader be eager to look for that day when such like institutions become quite common in India?

Indian Universities Act.—The various Universities are governed by the provisions of this Act. Its cursory perusal would show that the Act is bureaucratic in design. Though the Universities are autonomous bodies, yet they are under the control of the provincial governors who are their chancellors. The students are not given any representation in the Senate or Syndicate which are the legislative and executive bodies of a University. There are dilatory provisions for the registration of graduates. Only a graduate of ten years' standing can be registered as a voter for the University constituency.

Then there is a very strange provision for cancellation of degrees on subsequent behaviour. It is quite ununderstandable why should subsequent behaviour come in for consideration when a person was quite competent and of good behaviour at the time of conferring a degree upon him? Strange to say, that this provision is put into practice to cancel the degrees of those who in any way show their inclination to take or actually take interest in the political activities of the country.

CHAPTER VIII

ORIGIN OF STUDENT MOVEMENT IN INDIA

NO definite time can be assigned to the origin of the student movement in India. We are not much concerned with the student movement of the ancient or mediæval India. There was not so much of class consciousness prevalent then. The modern student movement might have originated under the influence of patriots like Sir Syed Ahmad and Raja Ram Mohan Roy, the two greatest reformers of their time, who did much for the spread of education. We know of some consciousness among students in 1884 when they protested against the holding of the I. C. S. competition in England.

The student movement was limited only to consciousness. This consciousness received a fillip in Maharashtra under the influence of Lokmanya Tilak and in Bengal by its Partition in 1905. Sir Gurdas Bannerji and Sri Aurobindo Ghose played a prominent part in the Bengal student movement. The Bengalee students as a protest against the Partition of Bengal left schools and colleges. They advocated the cause of Swadeshi. This movement became quite strong and ultimately succeeded. During this very period Lajpat Rai and Ajit Singh played a prominent part to arouse the students in the Punjab. Both of them were deported because they were suspected to lead some revolution. It may be remembered that their deportation took place just after a big conference at Lyallpur where S. Ajit Singh was a school teacher. In this conference the students participated in thousands.

It must be understood that then were no regular student organizations then. But the students being not immune from the external circumstances, allied themselves with national forces whenever any opportunity arose.

The second phase of the student activities was visible after 1919 during the Rowlatt Act agitation and the first Gandhian non-violent non-co-operation. There came repression and suppression in the wake of the Great War. All the expectations of the Indians for any constitutional advancement were belied. The Rowlatt Act Day was celebrated throughout the country and the students organized processions and *hartals*. In 1921 Gandhiji launched the first Civil Disobedience movement. He exhorted students to leave schools and colleges and actively participate in this campaign. The students generally responded to this call and vacated their classroom. The regime of Martial Law in the Punjab brought the Punjab students more close. National colleges were started at Lahore and Aligarh while Vidyapiths were established at Benares and Gujrat.

It was during this time that students felt the need of an independent and separate student organization. Some student unions were established in Bengal and Mahrashtra. These organizations were for the purpose of bringing students together on a common platform. These organizations discussed the topics of the day and identified themselves with them when any need arose. There are no traces of class consciousness then. After 1923 the student movement was dormant again.

It was in 1927 that the first real student organization was brought into existence in India. Bhagat Singh, Bhagwati Charn, Sukhdev and Ihsan Ilahi were its pioneers. They realized the potentialities of an independent student organization. They wanted to establish student unions throughout the province. They met with a great success in this direction. The first Lahore Students' Conference under the presidentship of the late Lala Lajpat Rai attracted students in thousands. Other provinces followed the example of the Punjab and organized local student organizations.

These student organizations mobilized the students on their general demands. Moreover,

ONE OF THE FOUNDERS

OF

THE STUDENT MOVEMENT IN THE PUNJAB

Virendra, M.A., Lahore

Govind Ballabh Pant, the U. P. Premier, addressing Lucknow Students

PROMINENT STUDENT WORKER

M. N. M. Badi-ud-Din, President, U. P. Students' Federation

1936-37

there was not much cohesion in these organizations. They worked locally and did not like to interfere or participate in the activities of students at other places.

The year 1930 witnessed the second Non-co-operative movement. There was once again a call for sacrifice. The student organizations welcomed it. Students led processions, organized *hartals*, and courted imprisonments. More than 250 students in the Punjab and even a larger number in Bengal, U. P. and Bombay were put behind the bars. The Punjab Students' Union, and student organizations in Bengal and Bombay were declared unlawful. This state of unrest continued up to 1933.

This struggle marked another land-mark in the national history of India. The country gained many lessons from it. Out of the vague and hazy notions of sacrifice and Swaraj, developed a scientific thinking. The socialist ideas of class consciousness became more visible and appeared more realistic.

In 1934 there came into existence Student Unions, almost at every important educational centre. Student Conferences were held at various places. It was for the first time that the students understood the importance of class-organization. The students were united on the slogans of: " Students unite to know and protect your rights". Since then the nation had not to launch on any mass movement. The student organizations got perfectly smooth times to organize and to strengthen themselves.

Though there came into existence many important student organizations like the Punjab Students' Union and the U. P. Students' Federation, yet no effort was made upto 1935 to link them into an All-India organization.

It was during the close of 1935 that Messrs. Badiuddin and Prem Naryan Bhargava of the U.P. Students' Federation issued circular letters to various provincial and local student organizations proposing the formation of an All-India Student organization. Their proposal was agreed to readily. It was in August, 1936 that the 1st All-India Students' Conference was convened at Lucknow. This Conference established the All-India Students' Federation. Students from the Punjab, U. P., C. P., Bengal, Assam, Bihar and Orissa attended this Conference.

So it was in fact in 1936 that a powerful and organized student movement in India was established and manifested in the All-India Students' Federation.

CHAPTER IX

STUDENT ORGANIZATIONS IN INDIA

THE first and the foremost student organization in India is the All-India Students' Federation. It has branches throughout India. It is a mass organization and attracts students of all shades and opinions. The growth and activities of this organization shall be dealt with in detail in the next chapter.

Then there are University Unions. They are not democratic bodies and are brought into existence simply to eulogize the University and its activities. These Unions attract very few students. But at places like Lucknow and Allahabad some progressive students have captured these Unions too. They have forced the authorities to introduce democratic principles and to accede to the various demands of students. For instance, these Unions have hoisted the national flag on the University buildings and have published progressive articles in the University Magaznies. Generally the activities of these Unions are confined to academic lectures, debates and indoor games.

There have grown some communal student

organizations also. The first among them is the Muslim Students' Federation. This organization came into existence a year after the establishment of the All-India Students' Federation. The pernicious move to divide the students on communal lines was conceived by some self-seeker communalists. The Muslim University Aligarh, the pioneer seat of Muslim learning, threw out this move and the University Union passed a resolution of solidarity of all the students under the All-India Students' Federation. In face of this strong opposition, a few workers of the Muslim Students' Federation held a meeting in *camera* and conducted their elections. None has felt its existence after that. It was a still-born organization, which is infused with some life only on some opportune or selfish occasions. One of its aims is to establish an Islamic empire, which has nothing to do directly with the popular demands of students.

Then there come other communal organizations like the Hindu Vidyarthi Sabha and Christian Students' Brotherhood. These organizations confine themselves to communal and secular activities. But now they are unheard of for a long time. It appears they have died a natural death in this age of class-consciousness, when communalists find ground slipping under their feet.

CHAPTER X

ALL-INDIA STUDENTS' FEDERATION

THE All-India Students' Federation is the only student organization in India under whose banner the students all over the country unite. It is a non-communal, non-sectarian organization and brings together students of every colour, shade or opinion. During a short existence of three years it has become a very powerful organization. It has branches all over India, from Kashmir to Ceylon on one side and from Karachi to Burma on the other. Its membership has run into many thousands.

Origin.—The All-India Students' Federation was the outcome of the efforts of the U. P. Students' Federation which strived to link the various provincial student organizations on an all-India basis, for the purpose of co-ordinating the struggle of hundreds of thousands of Indian students in schools, colleges and universities for liberty, culture and peace. The first All-India Students' Conference met at Lucknow in August, 1936. Nine hundred and eight-six delegates came from 210 local and 11 provincial organizations to attend this session. It was a Conference in the real sense of the word. There was no show, and there were no demonstrations. The delegates exchanged their views in a very calm and deliberative atmosphere. They talked and discussed with responsibility. The discussions continued till late at night and then were resumed early in the morning. The 'aims and objects' took at least two days. A section of the delegates wanted that the organization should take active part in politics, while the other opined that the political activities would restrict the basis, and the Federation would not develop into a mass organization. Pandit Jawahar Lal who opened this Conference and Mr. M. A. Jinnah who presided over the session gave their own suggestions. At last there was a compromise and the aims and objects incorporated the two divergent views in a consistent form.

Aims and objects.—The aims and objects of the All-India Students' Federation are :—

(*i*) to encourage cultural and intellectual co-operation on equal terms between the students of various provinces and Indian States, and between students of India and other parts of the world ;

(*ii*) to suggest improvements in the present system of education ;

(*iii*) to safeguard the rights of the student community ;

(*iv*) to prepare the students for citizenship, in order to take their due share in the struggle for complete national freedom, by arousing their political, social and economic consciousness.

Thus where the 'Federation' on the one hand wants to unite students on their common grievances, on the other it wants to arouse a political consciousness among them to prepare them to take their due share in the country's struggle for complete national freedom.

Conferences.—The first All-India Students' Conference was held at Lucknow in August, 1936. It continued its deliberations for four days and brought into existence the All-India Students' Federation. Pandit Jawahar Lal Nehru opened the Conference and Mr. M. A. Jinnah presided. Both of these leaders exhorted the students to make the organization powerful and to keep it free from communalism the bane which has been eating into the vitality of the nation. Mr. Prem Narain Bhargava was the chairman of the Reception-Committee. A provisional working committee with Mr. Bhargava as the General Secretary was elected unanimously.

This Conference also felt the necessity and desirability of starting some official organ to:

(*i*) ventilate the grievances of students, to support their cause and to organize them into a powerful organization;

(*ii*) seek to solve the problem of unemployment;

(*iii*) inuclcate the spirit of simple living and high thinking;

(*iv*) agitate against the drab system of education.

Mr. Prabodh Chandra, President of the Punjab Students' Federation took this arduous task upon himself. The *Students' Tribune*, the official organ of the All-India Students' Federation made its first appearance in November, 1936 under his editorship. Since then the *Students' Tribune* has grown into one of the first-class literary journals of India. It publishes articles on various student topics and gives a wide publicity to the activities of various student organizations.

The Second All-India Students' Conference met at Lahore under the presidentship of Sjt. Sarat Chandra Bose during November, 1936. Mr. Prabodh Chandra was the Chairman of the Reception Committee. This Conference was called only after three months, because it was to adopt the constitution and take stock of the organizational activities during this period. After three days' full discussion the Conference adopted a constitution which recognized the principle of presidium.

At this very Conference was adopted a "Charter of Student Demands".

The Third All-India Students' Conference met at Madras during the X'mas of 1937 under the presidentship of Mr. M. R. Massani. Mr. Haider Beg was the Chairman of the Reception Committee. This session witnessed a cleavage of thought among the various delegates. A section of delegates thought that a progressive group must predominate the Federation, while the other wanted to steer clear of any ideology or outside influence. The differences became so acute that the two groups held separate elections and Mr. Massani had to dissolve the session. However, better counsels prevailed. Soon after, due to the efforts of Dr. Ashraf, Mr. Massani and Sjt. Subhas Babu, the two groups united once again to carry on the work jointly and smoothly.

Activities.—The All-India Students' Federation primarily aims to unite students on their common grievances. It has organized many processions, strikes and marches to ventilate their grievances. Not only that, the Federation takes a keen interest in Indian and international problems. Its various organizations celebrated the All-India Prisoners' Day, All-India Detenues' Day, Spain Week and China Day. The detailed activities in various provinces are given in the succeeding chapters.

CHAPTER XI

STUDENT MOVEMENT IN THE PUNJAB

THOUGH the student movement in its organized form is of a recent origin in this province, yet spasmodic student activities can be traced as far back as 1905. During this year there was a strike in the King Edward Medical College, Lahore. It was perhaps the first student strike in India. It was led by Dr. Satya Pal now the President of the Punjab Provincial Congress Committee. Some racial discrimination between the English and the Indians gave rise to this strike. The self-respecting students could not tolerate this distinction. The students won a complete victory. This was the first signal success for any student campaign in India.

The Student Movement in the Punjab for the first time as such, drew its inspiration from the enactment of the 'blessed' Rowlatt Act in 1919. Hence before no tangible effort was ever made to organize the students in the sense, we understand it today. The establishment of the D. A.-V. College in the late ninetees, followed by the Dyal Singh College and other denominational institutions in the Province, developed a national-cum-communal consciousness which later in 1919 worked as a basis for national movement on broader lines. No doubt late L. Lajpat Rai, late L. Dawarka Dass, L. Sain Das and Mahatma Hans Raj with the active co-operation of men like Bhai Parma Nand of the D. A.-V. College group and Sardar Dyal Singh and others from the Brahmu Samaj did all what they could to inculcate the spirit of patriotism, simplicity and self-sacrifice among the student community. We are at present referring to the efforts made in this direction in the late 19th and early 20th centuries. We are told that L. Lajpat Rai regularly used to go round the rooms of the students in the Boarding Houses and would personally come in their contact by discussing matters of public and national importance. His lionian speeches thoroughly saturated, with sterling nationalism are still ringing in the ears of the students of those times. Biographies of men like Maizini, Garibaldy and Shivaji were adopted as study courses in the class-rooms.

But with all that, it still did not assume the proportions which were witnessed in the year 1919 and onwards. No doubt the students of those days ; especially those who came in contact with the late L. Lajpat Rai even now, visualize the atmosphere of almost aggressive nationalism then prevailing. If L. Lajpat Rai had not been deported and taken away from the field of his activities, it is universally agreed that the Punjab would have had a widespread student movement much earlier.

In 1919, the Government of India announced its intention of placing the Rowlatt Bill on the Statute Book. How vigorously the entire country protested, is now a matter of world history. Apart from the huge public demonstrations made in every nook and corner of the country by the public generally, the student community of the Punjab in particular lent their unstinted support to the widespread national protest. Lahore, the capital of the Province, is one of the biggest educational centres of the world. Here the student community almost went into a non-violent revolt. The intensity of the enthusiasm and national fervour displayed by the students during the months of February, March and April, 1919 shook the Government to its very foundations. A nation of volunteer corpse wholly composed of the students was formed. The city of Lahore appeared to be in the state of war. On roads, in gardens, streets, in fact everywhere groups of students were seen shouting national slogans, calling upon the people to realize the grave national danger lying ahead. The Government under the Lieutenant Governorship of the British hero, Sir Michael O'Dwyer was taking all possible measures to subdue this great "rising". Aeroplanes for the first time were requisitioned as a means to overawe the civil population. The then students in schools and colleges at Lahore still remember how these 'planes would hover over the buildings of the colleges and boarding houses late at night and how the students would leave their beds and shout their utter condemnation of the British policy. Huge student meetings were organized and very strong resolutions carried through with remarkable unanimity.

Anxious days and nights rolled on. Badshahi Mosque became the scene of huge public meetings where members of every community assembled. On one fateful day sometime in the afternoon, when some students in a group were coming after attending the meeting at Badshahi Mosque, they were stopped by the Police and an Honorary Magistrate and were assaulted. One of the students, Khushi Ram by name, was fired at seven times but that valient soldier of the motherland did not move an inch and with the eighth shot dropped down in pool of blood. But it is significant that not one shot was received by Khushi Ram on his back. The writer himself saw the dead body when it was taken to the cremation ground. The bullets had perforated his chest and it appeared a sort of garland resting on it.

This incident, first of its type, enraged the student community very much. But still the philosophy of Mahatma Gandhi had already taken its hold and no violent repurcussion was noticed. Huge protest meetings were held. Students refused to go to the colleges and schools and joined the processions which walked through the streets of Lahore.

It must be added, that the movement did not confine itself to Lahore alone, but it engulfed the entire Province. Schools and colleges out of Lahore were all ablaze and there was not a student who directly or indirectly did not join.

Then came the fateful firing at the Jallianwala Bagh at Amritsar followed by the enactment of the Martial Law. The Military began to rule the entire Province. The first attack was on the educational institutions. The students were asked to go to the particular places four times during the day, to get their presence noted to the Military authorities. During those hot summer months some of them were obliged to walk more than 15 miles a day. Their only conveyances, the push bycycles, had been already requisitioned by the Military under orders. Indiscriminate arrests were made out of whom some were sentenced to long terms of imprisonment, and if our recollection is correct a few of them were hanged at Kasur. Hundreds of students were expelled from the University. Thousands of them were fined and many were mercilessly flogged. Some of them got escaped from the Martial Law regime at Lahore but had to walk hundreds of miles on foot to their distant homes. The students of the Sanatan Dharam College Hostel about 250 in number were arrested in a body and were taken to the Lahore Fort carrying their beddings and other luggage on their own shoulders for a distance of about seven miles. There are numerous stories of the Martial Law repression directed against the students which for want of space cannot be incorporated in the present report.

Martial Law regime came and was withdrawn. Colleges were closed and re-opened. But everyone was smarting under the shadow of these black days. Although depressed due to the privations suffered by them, the students had created a different platform for themselves. They had proved to the world that the student community was a very potent factor in the fight for freedom. Mahatma Gandhi took its clue and in his 1920 non-cooperation programme he exhorted them to come out of the colleges.

The late L. Lajpat Rai by now had been permitted to come back to Punjab from his lengthy exile in America. He reached Lahore on the 24th of February, 1920. The appeal of the two Martial Law prisoners of Amritsar against their death sentence was announced to have been rejected by the Privy Council, the same day. All public arrangements for the reception of L. Lajpat Rai had to be cancelled, but still the students mustered strong at his residence and gave him a thundering ovation. Here had come back the guiding star of the student community. After the Nagpur Congress in the December 1920, the late L. Lajpat Rai rekindled the patriotic fervor of the students. He called upon them to leave their colleges and join the national army. It had its effect. They left and joined. He founded a National University for their instruction. Colleges were picketed, strikes were resorted to and no pursuation of the College authorities would bring their scholars back. They were holding their meetings in gardens, public halls and public thoroughfares. Seditious Meetings Act was declared in Lahore and meetings were prohibited. Students walked down to Gujranwala Town at a distance of over 40 miles to attend the Students' Conference held amidst scenes of unprecedented enthusiasm. And so the years rolled on. The engine of repression was taking every leader worth the name to different jails and none was left to guide the student community.

In the 1924 L. Lajpat Rai was released shattered in health. For one long year he could not actively participate in the politics on account of the rotten condition of his health, due to the prolonged ill-treatment in jail. In 1925 he came out of the

Aung San, President (*seated in centre*)

PROMINENT STUDENT WORKERS

Babubhai Jashbhai Patel, a student M. L. A.

D. N. Chibber, Prominent Worker of Rawalpindi Students' League

sick chamber and the students rallied round him. In the meanwhile the student community was rendering all possible support to the non-co-operation and civil disobedience movements. They had not forgotten the miseries of the foreign rule experienced by them in 1919. They were now badly in need of their own platform and a regular organization. Dhanwantri, recently repatriated from Andamans and now serving his long term of imprisonment in the Central Jail, Lahore, with the active co-operation of some of his comrades, majority of whom had to go through the jail ordeal at one time or the other, and with the blessings of the elder generation of the leaders, on the 4th November 1927 founded the Lahore Students' Union. The Union immediately took in hand the various problems confronting the students and in a very brief period became a very strong body. Suffocated meetings were held at very short intervals and they became a power in the body politics.

During those days the British Parliament had inflicted a Royal Commission on India to make recommendation regarding the new constitution to be introduced in India. Such a commission having no Indian on its personnel, was universally boycotted in India. Students again rallied round the flag of this Boycott Movement and huge demonstrations were held. The Simon Commission was to visit Lahore on the 30th October

1928. Section 144 of the Code of Criminal Procedure had been declared by which meetings, demonstrations and processions were prohibited. L. Lajpat Rai came down from Lucknow to defy this unjust order and led a huge procession to the Railway Station. The processionists were stopped by a barbed wire barricade. They sat down forming themselves into a meeting which was addressed by leaders. They were all peaceful when some British Police Officers came and tried to push back the crowd. L. Lajpat Rai was just near the barricade and was mercilessly beaten by one of those officers. We may add that considerable number of students had left their colleges and had joined the procession. The beating of L. Lajpat Rai was greatly resented to and the crowd was willing to take the law in their hands. But tactful handling by the leaders saved the situation. The crowd came back in a procession and met in a huge meeting addressed by L. Lajpat Rai. He declared that the beating was the last nail in the coffin of the British Empire. He exhorted the youngmen to do all what was in their power to liberate their country from the yoke of the foreign power. His own days, he announced at the top of his voice, were numbered, but he would die with a satisfaction that the youth of the country, for which he had laboured so hard throughout his life, would complete his mission.

And surprisingly enough, Lalaji quietly breathed his last 17 days after this speech. What a funeral procession ! what a youthful enthusiasm ! the world had rarely witnessed it before. The death of Lala Lajpat Rai was in fact the beginning of the revolutionary trend among the youth of the Province.

On the ashes of L. Lajpat Rai was built the revolutionary movement in the Nothern India. His death came as a clarion call to the youth of the country. He was the idol of the young. He loved them so dearly. His death coming as it did so soon after the police beating provoked the public and the police was openly and persistently charged as murderers of the great Leader.

Bhagat Singh, one of the students of the National College of Lahore founded by L. Lajpat Rai, by that time had definitely come in contact with the revolutionary party in India. He was long wanted by the police but was not available. He was in Central Provinces evading the police when he heard the tragic news about the death of Lala Lajpat Rai, under such tragic circumstances. His blood boiled. He had already flung away the non-violent philosophy of Mahatma Gandhi. He picked up his revolver and fired eight shots on the bare wall before him. Enraged, half dressed, he boarded the train for Cawnpore where he arranged an urgent meeting of his comrades. A unanimous decision was arrived at.

National insult in the death of Lala Lajpat Rai must be avenged and very soon. They reached Lahore, hired houses under fictitious names and surveyed the situation. On the 17th December, *i.e.*, 30 days after the death of Lala Lajpat Rai, one British Police Official, Saunders by name, coming out of the police Headquarters was shot dead and another Indian Officer, in an attempt to capture the assailants, too shared his fate. In the twinkling of an eye, police forces arrived on the scene of the murder. But the three young-men supposed to have been guilty of this grave offence had disappeared and even the best police search could not lay its hands upon them.

And then followed indiscriminate arrests of the students. The responsible officials of the Students' Union were clapped behind the iron bars. A panic prevailed. A large number of hands were requisitioned by the Criminal Investigation Department. In every College, every Hostel, in every educational institution these C. I. D. people were posted to watch. Even attempts were made to secure the services of some of the students for such a work. But assailants by now had reached Calcutta where the Congress was holding its Annual Session.

On the 8th April, 1929 when the Central Assembly was having its sitting in Delhi and the Trade Disputes Bill was moved for consideration, a bomb burst on the floor of the house followed by a few handbills entitling "Louder noise for the dumb to hear".

While the entire House was in the state of turmoil, two youngmen attired in Khaki were seen playing with pistols and shouting "Long Live Revolution" and "Down down with Imperialism", and smilingly offered themselves for arrest. The same month the police raided an Amateur Bomb Factory in Lahore and arrested three more youngmen.

Then came the famous trial of Bhagat Singh and his 18 compatriots arrested from all over India. This trial changed the entire phase of the student movement in the Punjab. Bhagat Singh and his comrades were absolutely indifferent to the consequences of the trial. They tried their utmost to use the Court as their propaganda platform. The prosecution and the Government with their tactless handling added fuel to the fire. Bhagat Singh and others caught the imagination of the public generally and the students particularly. Thousands of students would collect everyday outside the Jail Court precincts and shout revolutionary slogans, "Long Live Bhagat Singh" and "Long Live the Revolution". Every student had a photograph of Bhagat Singh in his room. Everyone was anxious to have a glimpse of him. In hostels and class-rooms, Bhagat Singh was the burning topic; and the time flowed on. The atmosphere in the colleges were rapidly becoming hostile to the philosophy of Non-violence. Youth had begun to develop a fancy for the cult of the bomb. Some very important members of the Students' Union were arrested and sentenced. Criminal Law Amendment Act came into operation and most of the youngmen were taken into custody.

On the other hand, the people were still agitating over the death of Lala Lajpat Rai. With Bhagat Singh in the Court and the shadow of Lala Laipat Rai staring in the face, some students actually joined the revolutionary camp. On the 23rd December 1929, the Viceregal Special carrying the Governor-General of India was electrically bombed, but none was seriously hurt.

On the 4th June 1930, early morning a bomb burst in a house at Lahore. It transpired later that it was a stronghold of the youthful revolutionaries who had hired that bungalow to rescue Bhagat Singh and others from the prisoners' van which used to carry them to the Court, near this bungalow. None could be arrested as the police arrived a little late. On the 19th June 1930, arrangement for the explosion of bombs at six different places in the Province were fixed up, out of which at two places it caused fatal injuries to the Police Officers. The party responsible for these outrages consisted mostly of youngmen, majority of whom were students. On the 30th of March 1931,

Bhagat Singh and his two comrades namely Sukh Dev and Raj Guru were hanged which raised another severe storm of protests.

The motive of the capital punishment is always deterrent. The existence of such a system is not justified in the modern criminal jurisprudence if it does not produce those feelings of awe and fear thus acting as a checkmate to the recrudence of the crime. But the death penalty imposed upon these three youngmen was considered as having been inflicted more in the interest of the prestige of the Punjab Bureaucracy rather than to satisfy the provision of the Criminal Law of India. During these very days Mahatma Gandhi and Lord Irwin, the Governor-General of India, were carrying on peace negotiations, which culminated into the Gandhi-Irwin Pact. The people thought that the death sentence imposed by the Court would be commuted to a lesser punishment. But guillotine news came as a blow and the whole of the student community along with the entire nation gave vent to their inner feelings of bitterness and resentment. Students refused to go to their classrooms and picketed the gates of the colleges and schools thus making it impossible for the teachers to go into the compounds even. Girl students along with boys were arrested, summarily convicted and sentenced to different terms of punishment.

In December 1931, when His Excellency the Governor of the Punjab was coming out of the University Hall after delivering the Convocation Address, a youngman politely drew his pistol off his sleeves and fired. His Excellency luckily did not get any serious injury. One Police Officer died. In connection with this outrage too, some very important members of the Students' Union were arrested and were sentenced to death by the Sessions Court but were acquitted in appeal by the High Court of Judicature on merits.

After having attended the Round Table Conference Mahatma Gandhi rerurned from England in January 1932. A definite rupture in the meanwhile had taken place between the Congress and the Government. The Gandhi-Irwin Pact had been mercilessly butchered. Pandit Jawaharlal and others had been arrested before the arrival of Mahatma Gandhi. He asked the Viceroy for an interview, which was refused without a blush. And so the Civil Disobedience attack was again launched. Hundreds of students in the Punjab joined the volunteer organization and were sent to prisons. Boycott of British Goods was resorted to.

Not only that the Students levishly made donations out of their own personal monthly expenses at different occasions of national importance. Quetta and Bihar Earthquake Funds were subscribed to by the students in thousands. Jatin Dass Fund and Bardoli Peasant Movement were given an ample financial support. In fact the students contributed to the national struggle much beyond the expectations.

After the second Civil Disobedience movement there came a lull in the political activities of the country as a whole. The students in the Punjab now had a good opportunity to re-organize their movement on a powerful and stronger basis. It was deemed desirable that to bring students of the province closer to each other a Provincial Students' Conference should be held at Lahore. A humble Reception Committee was formed. But it worked zeolously day and night. The result was that there was a great awakening among the students.

The Fifth Punjab Students' Conference was held during February, 1934. Dr. Rabindra Nath Tagore presided. Leaders of the eminence of Sjt. Bhulabhai Desai, Sarojini Naidu, Dewan Chaman Lal addressed the students. All roads of Lahore led to the Bradlaugh Hall where students thronged in thousands to hear these leaders and give proof of their solidarity under the Student Union. A poetical symposium was also held along with the Conference. Poets like Tagore, Sarojini Naidu, Josh Malihabadi, Saghir Nizami and Ihsan Bin Danish gave recitations befitting the occasion. More than twenty thousand persons attended this symposium. Bradlaugh Hall was packed to suffocation. This Conference has been unprecedented in the history of the student movement in India. The credit for its success goes to Mr. Prabodh Chandra, the then General Secretary of the Reception Committee who was the moving figure in this Conference.

The consciousness and the awakening created by this Conference was fully utilized by establishing Student Unions throughout the Province. Within a short span of six months powerful student organizations sprang up at Jullundur, Moga, Hoshiarpur, Ludhiana, Ferozepore, Gujranwala, Rawalpindi, Sailkot, Multan, Kapurthala, and Jammu.

In August 1936 a batch of the Punjab delegates went to Lucknow to attend the First All-India Students' Conference, convened by the U.P. Students' Federation. They took a keen interest in the discussions and gave their full co-operation to expedite the formation of the All-India Students' Federation. So much so that Mr. Prabodh Chandra took the sole responsibility of running the *Students' Tribune*—the official organ of the All-India Students' Federation. He invited the second session of the All-India Students' Conference at Lahore.

This momentous second session of the All-India Students' Conference was held in November, 1936 in the Bradlaugh Hall. Sjt. Sarat Chandra

Bose, the well-known youth leader of Bengal presided. This Conference adopted the constitution for the A. I. S. F. and a Charter of the Student demands.

During 1937 two events of historical importance took place in the student movement. They were the Khalsa College (Amritsar) and the Ayurvedic College (Lahore) strikes. These strikes continued for months, together. They would be treated in detail in a separate chapter. Suffice it to say that students led by Mr. Prabodh Chandra, the President of the Punjab Students' Federation achieved a unique success in these two strikes. Almost all of their demands were acceded to.

Apart from their quota to the struggle of liberty which they amply contributed, the Students of the Punjab have all along been taking co-operative measures to improve their own lot as students. Regularly they had been holding Conferences, adopting resolutions concerning the University and its curriculum, celebrating definite weeks to study and tackle particular subjects, making thoughtful representations about Examinations and their methods. In fact the Student Union has in these few years covered a very wide range of varied subjects and has done much useful work in the interest and for the benefit of the students.

Student movement the in Punjab has definitely come to stay. Their chief organization is a representative body satisfying different interests. They have rendered unique services to the cause of the country and the nation. An average student to-day is superior to his brother of yesterday. He is more alive to his rights and duties and is better conscious of environments around him.

We make bold so say that the student movement has contributed more to the betterment of the student community than all the efforts of the University as a teaching media. This movement has raised the students to a higher level of thought and action. It has infused in them a spirit of independence which was purposely divorced from the system of education. The class-rooms in Punjab only provide instructions in different subjects to merely enable the students to appear in the UniversityExaminations. The student movement has furnished the real aim of education. With the progress of time and given more opportunities, we hope, the student movement will rapidly march forward and will be more useful to the students and the country.

CHAPTER XII

STUDENT MOVEMENT IN U. P.

THE U. P. students took part in the two Non-co-operation movements of 1921 and 1930. The political conditions during 1929 brought about a wide awakening amongst the students. Despite this consciousness there was no student organization worth the name. Students joined the Youth movements like the Naujawan Bharat Sabha and the Tarun Sangh. It was after the second Civil Disobedience movement, that some student organizations came into existence. The various organizations were further linked up in the U.P. Students' Federation. The activities these organizations had been more or less educational, arranging lectures and debates on various political, economic and social topics.

The United Provinces have been the centre of unprecedented activities in the student circles since the formation of the All-India Students' Federation. Students became more alive to their responsibilities and privileges. In a couple of months after the establishment of the All-India Students' Federation, Student Unions were formed at Lucknow, Cawnpore, Allahabad, Aligarh Bareilly, Meerut, Dehradun, Khurja and Barabanki.

The outstanding activities during 1936 had been the Muslim University Aligarh strike and the fate of the proposed All-India Muslim Students' Federation.

The Aligarh Strike.—In October, 1936 some students of the Muslim University were expelled for some alleged misbehaviour. In fact these students attracted the attention of the University authrities by rousing a national spirit amongst the students; but the authorities expelled them under the pretext of misbehaviour. The students could easily understand the motive behind this uncalled-for action of the University authorities. They could not sacrifice their progressive colleagues so very easily. They went on strike which compelled the authorities to close down the institution for the Dussehra holidays much before time. The students stayed on and the authorities had even to pay their railway fares to send the students to their homes. On the re-opening of the University the authorities had to take back the expelled students before peace was restored in the University.

The All-India Students' Conference.—In the second important event of the year too, the Muslim Students acquitted themselves most creditably by turning down the proposal for the formation of an All-India Muslim Students' Federation.

Just after the first session of the All-India Students' Conference at Lucknow certain people took it upon themselves to foster communal feelings amongst the united ranks of the students of this country. These people were but some communalist Mohamedan leaders. In November 1936 was moved a resolution, in the Aligarh Muslim University Union, for the formation of the All-India Muslim Students' Federation. This proposal was turned down in an overwhelming majority unprecedented in the history of the Union. The Muslim students of that centre of Islamic culture well exhibited the glory of Islam by showing their national spirit and their disregard of this policy of creating rancour and ill-will between the two sister-communities of the Indian Nation. Uundeterred by this unforeseen defeat, the convener of the proposed All-India Muslim Students' Conference carried on his propaganda for this un-called for sectarian move and went around the country to enlist support. At Lucknow was invited the 1st All-India Muslim Students' Conference, with A. Yusuf Ali as the president-elect. But the persistent opposition of the nationalist Muslim students of this country made it impossible for him to hold this conference on the announced date. In place of that Conference, the delegates assembled at Lucknow and passed a unanimous resolution dissociating themselves from this sectarian move. They placed their full confidence in the All-India Students' Federation.

The elections to the Provincial Legislature under the new Act gave a new impetus to the movement in February, 1937. The students throughout the province helped the Congress in these elections by acting as polling agents and convassers and acquitted themselves well. This attitude of the students led to their victimization by the educational authorities and the students had to go on strike to preserve their rights and privileges against the uncalled for authoritarianism. At Fyzabad the students were ordered not to attend the lecture of Mrs. Sorajini Naidu. Some students who defied the order were fined Rs. 2 each. The students went on strike against this order. Better counsels prevailed and the Principal withdrew his order after a days strike.

At Cawnpore, the Principal of the D. A.-V. College issued an order prohibiting the resident students from going to the polling booths and working in the elections. A few days later, the Principal suspended the concessions and stipends of some students. The students tried to approach the Principal ; but he did not see them and they were compelled to go on strike. The students of the B.Sc. class did not appear in the Final examination and supported the strike.

After a week's strike the Principal withdrew his orders unconditionally and the strike was called off. Calling off the strike the students by a resolution affirmed their right to take part in politics.

Student organizations at Meerut, Aligarh, Allahabad and Benares were quite active in the beginning of the year 1937.

In August 1937 were arrested Messrs. Romesh Chandra Sinha (Allahabad) and J. Bhattacharya (Benares) the two zealous workers of the U. P. Students' Federation. They were charged under Section 17(1, 2) of the Criminal Law Amendment Act. The students held meetings throughout U. P. and outside to protest against these arrests. They wanted that the Congress which was in office and which was committed to the policy of freedom of thought, speech and association must release these two student-workers.

At Jhansi the students celebrated Palestine Day and distributed pamphlets in connection with that. One of the student workers was caned for this. The students decided to go on strike till the authorities expressed regret. After a couple of days' strike the authorities had to yeild, promising that there would be no victimization. During this period the students of Ranikhet in a meeting condemned the unwarranted attack made by Lord Baden Powell, the chief scout, on Indian morality, culture and character. It called upon the students to totally boycott the Boy Scout Movement and join the Sewa Samiti Boy Scouts Association.

The U. P. Students' March.—In October, 1937, a mile long procession of fifteen thousand students from all parts of the United Provinces headed by Mr. Prem Narayan Bhargava, the then General Secretary, A. I. S. F., after parading the main streets of Lucknow marched to the house of Pandit Gobind Vallabh Pant, the U. P. (Congress) Premier, in order to place before him their grievances and demands passed by the All-India Students' Federation at its Lahore Session.

The demands numbered 37, important among them being the re-admission of three students in their higher classes in the Aligarh University, who were refused admission for the alleged participation in the activities of the Students' Federation and if the University failed to do, the Government should stop its grant, withdrawal of cases against Messrs. Sinha and Bhattacharya who were arrested for the alleged possession of the communist literature, two promotion examinations within one year, abolition of detention clause, and percentage of attendance like the foreign Universities. While putting the demands before the Premier it was impressed upon him that there was no communalism in the students' ranks. The students organized the March to show that the All-India Students' Federation was a real representative body.

Pandit Gobind Vallabh Pant replying said that their demands were in nature of commands. The Ministers and Congress leaders, he said, like good fathers, would do everything in the interest of their sons, who should leave the granting of demands to them. He congratulated the members of the Federation for abolishing communalism. He placed before them the idea of Mahatma Gandhi—which was service to country and non-violence. The Premier advised the students not to hanker after jobs but work in the villages.

The students while thanking the Premier, asked how the students could develop their intelligence and health when they had nothing to eat. The Federation, they informed, had implicit faith in the Congress government but requested the Ministers also to listen to their grievances and not depend merely on the authorities' version.

The end of October witnessed the two important events in this province—the U. P. Students' Conference and the Lucknow Medical School strike. During this period the organizational work was taken more seriously. Student organizations were established at almost all important educational centres. The membership of the U. P. Students' Fedration increased to many thousands.

The U. P. Students' Federation has been identifying itself fully with the activities of the All-India Students' Federation. It sent more than a score of delegates to the Lahore and the Madras Sessions. The U. P. Students' Federation is maintaining the office of the All-India Federation since its very inception. Messrs. Prem Narayan Bhargava ex-General Secretary and Ansar Harvani the present General Secretary of the All-India Students' Federation belong to the U. P. Students' Federation. So the U. P. Students' Federation has so far the unique distinction of holding this important office. Aligarh, the important Muslim educational centre, maintains the office of the Informatiom Bureau of the All-India Students' Federation.

CHAPTER XIII

STUDENT MOVEMENT IN BENGAL

BY virtue of their plasticity, receptiveness and high-strung emotions, students are bound to play a revolutionary role in the national struggle. They must form the backbone of any aggressive movement. In Bengal, students have never failed to play their part in the freedom movement. In the Civil Disobedience of 1930, they formed the vanguard of the army.

The student movement was then in Bengal, an auxiliary to the national struggle, raging in full swing at that period. The movement itself was in a formless state. It could not be said to possess a separate entity. It was caught, in spite of itself, in the vortex of forces, inevitably pushed forward by a momentum of its own. The leadership was in other's hands. Only very rarely, students directed the movement on their own lines, chalking out a distinctive course of action. But they put up a splendid show. Thousands of them marched to jail or the concentration camps and faced the *lathi* charges. Schools and colleges were boycoted. "Education can wait," it was said, "But *Swaraj* cannot."

Expectations were pitched high. Students set to work with taut nerves and set faces. It was a glorious chapter in the history of the nation. Students, on their part, could legitimately be proud of their brave doings.

Gradually, the first flush of enthusiasm wore off. Though the movement continued for sometime in a lower key, it was no more possible to recapture the first mood of care-free idealism. In Bengal, as elsewhere, a period of lull and inaction came. This interlude was very painful. Students tried to eschew politics, because the engine of repression knew no rest,—it relentlessly drove on. They fell into a soft and pointless existence. They grew lackadaisical, taking only a languid interest in the events of the day. Their morale had gone low. Most of the leaders being inside the prison bars, none was there to communicate any political stimulus to the student community.

Both A. B. S. A. and B. P. S. A. were under ban. At this stage, Mrs. Sarojini Naidu inaugurated the Students' Radical Party. It contested the election of the Under-Secretaries of the Calcutta University Institute. It also took upon itself the task of toning up the political mentality of students. It organised meetings and processions. It conducted occasional strikes in colleges. The Institute-programme of the Party has been eminently successful. It has been capturing all the seats for the last four years.

About two years later, the All-Bengal Students Conference was held and the Bengal Provincial Students' League formed. The lull was gradually passing. Students were slowly coming to their own.

Soon after, the All-India Students' Conference met at Lucknow. The Provincial Conference was held in October, 1937 and the B. P. S. F. born. Under this body, the different groups attained a cohesion and unity hitherto lacking. By this time, the period of reaction and inertness was over. Students had gained back much that seemed to be lost and crushed—resiliency, spirit of adventure, 'pep'. There came a new awareness in them. They grew conscious of their role. They responded now to the call heartily. It is unnecessary to recount the activities of the present year, for they have been regularly reported in the *Students' Tribune*, the official organ of the All-India Students' Federation.

It is permissible to take advantage of this occasion to offer some reflections on the present day student movement in Bengal. Like other movements of similar nature, it has its phases, its ups and downs, its rise and fall. It is to a great extent dependent on the general temper of the country. It varies according to the political ebb and flow.

Bengal has not yet developed steady leadership. Though it possesses rich emotional content, it is sometimes vacillating, wobbling, hesitant, irresolute. Sometimes it overshoots the mark and gloats over its own sabotage. It is often carried away by washy sob-stuff. It must rid itself of a lapse into talking through the hat and irresponsible high-falutin, punctuated by a lavish use of jargon, thereby giving a handle to Imperialism. The student movement must know its direction and purpose. A grip over the tempo of action must be established. The present-day students of Bengal possess marvellous materials for leadership. It can be hoped that with the accretion of experience, the movement will evolve the right type of leadership best suited to its growth and development.

The most important event of 1937 was the magnificent rally of the students in support of the Andamans hunger-strikers. The spontaneity of it was amazing. Leaders seemed to be pitchforked into their positions, being engulfed in a surge of enthusiasm. It revived the memory of the Civil Disobedience days. The whole atmosphere was electric. All groups put their heads together and coalesced with the B. P. S. F. The movement gained daily in intensity and volume. Students recked little of the consequences and chose to disregard the warning given by mature politicians, our war-worn and war-wise veterans. The *lathi*-charge and arrests only served to make the movement stupendous in proportions. But it was not canalized for effective purposes and was allowed to overflow. The result was that with the suspension of the hunger-strike and even before that, the ebb-tide set in. It did one great thing. It lent great prestige to the Students' Federation and increased the number of clientele, thus helping its organisational work. But due to effervescence, full advantage could not be taken of the movement.

The movement is very propitious to-day for strengthening the student movement. The student community is no longer blessed with a large store of philosophic content. Old ideas have tumbled down. It is very conscious and displays a great deal of mental agility. It has become critical, wary and suspicious. Authoritarianism is its pet aversion. Students are no longer prepared to recognise the old values and are profoundly disatisfied with the present structure of acquisitive society where the barest justice is denied. They chafe at and rebel against the stifling rigidity of the existing institutions and are prepared to demolish them and raise better ones in their stead. The hope can be fulfilled only by creating unity and solidarity in their ranks, by adequate intellectual equipment and by fitting ideals with action. Empty verbiage leads no one anywhere. With the proper ideology should be added a clare for action.

The discussion of the dictum 'students should not join politics' *ad nauseum* makes one mad with rage and disgust. Almost every address to the students contains a homily on the point. Were the dictum true, by the widest possible stretch of imagination, the A. I. S. F. had better wind up its business. If a student carefully avoids politics, he stands a very good chance of blossoming into a reactionary at the earliest opportunity. It is practically sending him without rudder and compass, to shift for himself. Politics will make his hide stout, capable of standing hard nocks. In a dependency, where the feeling of subjection and national humiliation always rankles in one's heart, it is a mockery and imposture to ask one give politics a wide berth. How can one avoid thinking in terms of political independence and freedom from exploitations. When we are trying to rouse the political consciousness of the student community, the dictum definitely injures our cause and strengthens the hands of those we are fighting against. A student need not join aggressive politics—and in normal times none will ask him to—but he should certainly be expected to cast his vote on the right side.

CHAPTER XIV

STUDENT MOVEMENT IN MADRAS

BEFORE 1936 there was no student organizations in the presidency of Madras. The radical students worked in other labour and class organizations. Pandit Jawahar Lal Nehru paid a visit to Madras in November, 1936. His visit was an impetus to the radical group of students to rally their less courageous brethren into an organized body for collecting funds and for the spreading of socialism. The excellent work turned out on this occasion deserved self-appreciation and instilled into leaders a sense of confidence in the capacity of students to rise equal to the occasion. Two thousand rupees was the size of the purse presented to Pandit Nehru; but it represented the feelings of twenty thousand students. The occasion was taken by Pandit Nehru to advise the students on their duty to their fellow-countrymen.

The seeds of an organization were sown. It was a matter of time before this 'airy nothing took a shape' and was a given local habitation and a name. The organization was called the Madras Students' Organization. The Madras Students' organization was formed on the 10th January, 1937 at a well-attended gathering of the students of the city. The objects and aims were radical in instinct. Anti-sectarian, anti-Imperialist and other anti-reactionary policies were chalked out. Various committees were formed and enrolment began in right earnest. There is a progressive feature in the constitution of M. S. O. For the afficient working of the office-bearers and in order that they may not be hampered by red-tapism it, was decided to make away with the President. They were considered to better creations of reformist bodies for people who hanker after offices. The Central Council of representatives, the Executive Committee and various sub-Committees are the veins of the M. S. O.

In January, 1937 the Madras students accorded their appreciation of the Muslim Students of Aligarh with as sincere a heart as their protest against the enhancement of school fees in Madurantakam High School.

Later the students congratulated the Congress on its success in the recent elections, and avowed their support in its future anti-Imperialist struggle.

On the 1st August 1937, the M. S. O. took upon itself the responsibility of celebrating International Anti-War Day. In the evening processions were started from various educational centres which converged into a large procession.

This procession proceeded along the principal bazars with banners bearing slogans and terminated at Marina where a public meeting was held under the auspices of the Madras Students' Organization. At this meetsng the students expressed their determination to reject all imperialist wars.

The organization has been running various study classes in various parts of the city. In August, 1937 when the students heard of a brutal *lathi*-charge on a procession of the Bengal students, they atonce organized a huge procession from the various colleges and schools. It proceeded to the Congress House, where a big meeting was held under the auspices of a M. S. O. when speeches were made condemning *lathi*-charge and resolutions were passed sympathising with the Bengal students and the Andamans hunger-strikers. The other day students of Vizagapatam went on strike as a protest against the non-recognition of their medical degrees. The M. S. O. led a deputation to the M.L.A.'s to put forth the Vizag students' grievances.

China Day was celebrated under the joint auspices of the M. S. O and the local Congress Socialist Party. A huge meeting was held at the Jawahar Ghat. The Vizag Students' Organization celebrated this day in a befitting manner. They issued a pamphlet : *Sino-Japanese War* on this occasion. At Trichinopoly the day was observed with a demonstration and a public meeting.

Comrade Batliwala was arrested at Tellichery as he was presiding over the third All-Malabar Students' Conference, under S. 124-I. P. C. for a speech at Nellore. Protesting against this arrest which was not only a volation of civil liberties but also obstrucious to student enterprize, circulars were issued to the organizations in the Presidency to protest against this arrest.

In October, 1937 a Conference of the students of Rayalascema was called forth at Mandanapalli. Dr. Pallabhi Sitaramyya presided on the occasion. During November and December intense propaganda was carried on in connection with the 3rd All-India Students' Conference.

This Conference was held at Madras during the Xmas. Comrade M. R. Massani presided over the delibrations. Messrs. Rama Rao and Haider Beg looked to the needs and comforts of the delegates who came from the whole length and breadth of the country. A progressive tendency seemed to gain an upper hand during the deliberations. Owing to some constitutional irregularities, the president dissolved the session. Unfortunately, a section of the students held new elections. But better senses prevailed after a short time. The students recognised the superiority of the All-India Students' Federation, and submerging all difference a unanimous working committee with Mr. Ansar Harvani (of Aligarh) as General Secretary was elected.

After the third All-India Students' Conference activities of the student organizations in the Presidency have been enlarged and many more organizations have been brought into existence.

CHAPTER XV

STUDENT MOVEMENT IN BOMBAY

THE entry of the Simon Commission in 1928 into India through the Bombay harbour may well be marked as the starting point of the political phase of the student movement in the Bombay Presidency. The said Commission was greeted with black flags and 'Simon go back' slogans, when it landed on the shores of India. Great demonstrations in the form of processions and meetings were held by the students.

Prior to this the Bombay students were carrying on social activities of going into the slum areas and teaching children, playing with them, advising adults on cleanliness and all sorts of social problems. The service in the slums and Harijan areas have been carried on ceaselessly by students till now. Students also went to the Blind School voluntarily to read to the poor blind brethren daily papers, stories and news of the world which perhaps they were never destined to know.

In 1929 the Youth League was organized in Bombay. In co-ordination with this organization the Bombay Students' Brotherhood, the oldest

PROMINENT STUDENT WORKERS

Prem Narayan Bhargava, Ex-Genl. Secy., All-India Students' Federation, 1936-37

Abdul Haye, President Khyber Union N.-W. F., 1937-38.

Balbir Sawhney, President Rawalpindi Students' League, 1936

Zafar Ullah, President Kapurthala Students' Union, 1937-38

PROMINENT WORKERS
OF
THE RAWALPINDI STUDENTS' LEAGUE

MOHAN LAL VINAYAK
Founder member of the Rawalpindi Students' Union

ZAFAR ALI
Pioneer of the Students' Movement in Rawalpindi

students' organization, launched a programme of study-circles, lectures and other such like activities. In the 1930 Civil Disobedience Movement the Youth League played a characteristic role and was soon declared illegal. The ban on it was removed only a few months ago. In all political agitations, propaganda and activities, this League was the premier youth organization with a band of brilliant student-workers. During the Civil Disobedience Movement street-corner meetings were organized. When a student or a big leader was arrested meetings of protests were held and *hartals* on all political days were observed. Picketing of foreign cloth and liquor shops was also carried on. But all these activities were not controlled by any organized student union. Stray hands of students put in their mite.

During the truce period the *Swadeshi* Movement was started in Bombay. In that also the students took a leading part by organizing the Bombay Students Swadeshi League. Under its auspices study circles were organized. They taught economics to the laymen and students. Statistics were gathered on various indigenous commodities. House to house propaganda for *Swadeshi* was carried on. *Swadeshi* article museums were organised. *Swadeshi* goods exhibitions were held. Lotus League was started to have a non-political but Swadeshi-minded membership. Moving exhibitions in lorries were organized and *Khadir*

Swadeshi articles were sold from house to house by the student volunteers.

With the historic fast of Mahatma Gandhi, the *Harijan* Movement started and the students did not lay behind in organizing the Students' Anti-Untouchable Committee. Propaganda meetings were held under its auspices. *Yagnas* were performed in the *Harijan* centres by the *Harijans* under its auspices. Census statistics were collected by the student volunteers. And in the referendum that was taken on the electorate question the students contributed their mite.

In all these activities the students held a position of respect with the merchant classes, the congress leaders, the Indian Merchants' Chamber, The Swadeshi League, and the Anti-Untouchability Committee started by Gandhiji. In the Civil Disobedience movements the records themselves speak of the students' fervour and zeal and we need not write much about it.

Till now the students platform remained an unorganized one having no organization of its own ; nor did the students realize their own difficulties. Stray attempts were made and the University reforms were demanded from various platforms but either they were not followed up, or resulted in nothing.

The Bombay City Students' Conference was organized but its voice remained a voice in the wilderness—though all the credit goes to it for awakening the student mass and bringing up a student ideology not in the city alone but in the whole of India. Its thesis was adopted by the All-India Students' Conference held at Lucknow for starting the A. I. S. F. But one sad feature of it was that it killed is own mother. The Bombay Students' Brotherhood which called the Conference, could not carry out the programme evolved at the Conference and we had to start another organization for conducting the activities. Brotherhood's death knell was rung. But, still, it survives and carries on its glorious work unstinted. All honour to it! All glory for having revitalized the student activities—by giving a new lead in a new direction.

The 1st All-India Students Conference at Lucknow evolved a Federation and we have traced the growth and development of the Federation in India in our students' mouthpiece the *Students Tribune*; so we need not mention anything here. But we feel proud of the line of work, the rapid growth and the energy spread among the student masses. In Bombay we have the Presidency Federation with about thirty primary units; and in the city three Unions of which the Bombay Students' Union (South) is the biggest and worthy of note. The Union has launched on a constructive programme for organizing the students and doing service to the Mother Country. We intend to start a hostel and a store run by students entirely and from its profits give poor students aid in the form of money for fees and books. We are launching the Literary Campaign in the villages with the blessings of great persons. We shall, responding to the call of the Congress President, start shortly a Volunteer Corps. We held a cinema show to gather funds for our activities, ran a stall in the Indian Industries Fair Exhibition. We are holding lectures, debates and all other activities to popularize our Union and the student movement. On behalf of the Union we join in all programmes conducted by the Congress and other progressive organizations with a view to make the student movement more and more popular and make its voice felt in the social and political affairs of our nation.

The Presidency Students' Federation is conducting training classes under proper guidance for our Literary Campaign. In short, the Bombay Presidency Students' Federation has grown into one of the premier organizations in India and is a great asset to A. I. S. F.

CHAPTER XVI

STUDENT MOVEMENT IN DELHI

THE history of the student movement in Delhi can be traced back to the year 1930. This was the year when the non-co-operation movement had been started by the Congress and thousands of men and women were courting arrests in connection with the salt *Satyagraha.* The students could not remain unaffected and formed a Students' Union at Delhi. It did a lot of work but was soon banned; its important office-bearers were arrested and thus it became extinct.

Again in the year 1933 when Gandhiji started his anti-untouchability compaign the students of Delhi felt a strong desire to organize themselves to ameliorate the condition of the *Harijans* of Delhi. Accordingly Students' Harijan Service League was formed with Mr. N. V. Thadani, Principal Hindu College as its president. The students were fortunate in having Seth G. D. Birla as its patron and the late Mr. B. S. Manyam Iyer as its Organizing Secretary. The league was very popular and did much useful work. It ran several day and night schools in the *Harijan* quarters and also conducted weekly tours in the *Basties* by the students. It also organized a sweeping demonstration by the students in the *Chandni Chowk* to illustrate the dignity of labour. When Gandhiji came on his *Harijan* tour in Delhi he was presented with a purse of Rs. 1,500 by the students of Delhi. The entire function was organized under the Harijan League and for the first time the professors and the students of the various colleges gathered together on one platform to pay their homage to the saint of Sabarmati and Sheogaon. The membership of the league swelled at this time to about 2,000. The entire student community of the Commercial and Ramjas colleges due to the active co-operation of its principals became its member. This attracted the attention of the local authorities and notices were served on Mr. R. P. Gupta and others to quit Delhi within 24 hours. The work continued unabated. Efforts were made to form a University Students' Union but proved abortive. No efforts were made after this to bring the students of various colleges on one platform, though the individual students continued to participate in social and political activities. Feelings of localism prevailed in different colleges.

Delhi Students' Federation.—This regrettable state of affairs continued till September, 1936 when Mr. K. P. Shankara the then Secretary of the University Law Union Society called a meeting of the representatives of the various colleges in St. Stephens College to discuss the ways and means of forming a Students' Federation in Delhi on the lines of the All-India Students' Federation. Happily Mr. Batliwala president-ellect of the Delhi Provincial Labour Conference happened to be in Delhi and he was invited to address the representatives about the lines on which the work should be done. Students were greatly impressed by what he said and decided to call a general meeting of the students in the Arabic College. The meeting was duly held on the announced date and Mr. Kanwar Lal and Mr. K. P. Shankara were unanimously elected as the President and the General Secretary respectively. The response in the beginning was not very encouraging but the work cantinued undaunted. A large number of functions were held, the important being the lectures of Mr. Mardyjones ex-M. P. and Mr. Asaf Ali, M. L. A. With a view to raise funds for the work a music competition and a drama were also organized. Both of them were a great success. The Federation also sent 15 delegates to the 2nd session of the All-India Students' Federation at Lahore. The Federation as well organized several village tours to establish personal contact with the villagers and understand their problems. In the villages the students distributed soap and encouraged the villagers to observe cleanliness, banish untouchability and send their boys to schools. To give a practical demonstration of their faith to remove untouchability they dined several times with the depressed classes of the villages and were thus able to create better feelings between the cast Hindus and the *Harijans.* During the All-India Convention held in March 1937 a good number of the members of the Federation acted as volunteers. The D. S. F. also Organized strikes in different Colleges of the Delhi University on 1st April as a protest against the new constitution according to the instructions of Mr. Prem Narayan Bhargava, then General Secretary A. I. S. F.

Delhi Students' Provincial Conference.—The year 1937 saw a distinct improvement in the interest of the students and the public, evinced in the activities of the Federation. On the 5th, 6th and 7th November a Provincial Students' Conference was organized by the Federation. Mrs. Kamladevi Chattopadhya presided while Sir Wazir Hasan delivered the inaugral address. The Conference continued for three days. It attracted a very large number of students and public to its sessions daily. The Conference passed a number of resolutions, the important being about the reduction in the fees of the Delhi University, starting a Gymnasium for the students, organizing a volunteer corps of the students and it called upon the students to resign from the scout movement as a protest against the remarks of Baden Powell about Indians. Other resolutions asking the Congress to oppose the coming Federation, sympathizing with the hunger strikers in the Andamans, etc., were also passed. Miss R. S. Naidu, Head Mistress of the Indra Prashta Girls' High School greatly helped the organizers by her co-operation during the Conference days. The Principal of the Commercial College was kind enough to close the College during the Conference days and thus enable the students to attend the Conference.

Village Work.—After 1937-38 elections, the newly elected committee soon after it took the charge, concentrated its attention mainly to the village work. A sub-Committee has been conducting village tours fortnightly. Besides the distribution of soap and medicines the members also explain to the villagers the advantages of sending their children to schools, organizing co-operative Societies and the evils of untouchability. So far the students have met with success in their efforts and the Federation is thinking of arranging a series of lectures on social, political and agricultural problems in the near villages in order to arouse in the villagers social, political and economic consciousness.

Strikes.—Two very important strikes occurred during 1937. The first strike called "Arabic Schools' Strike" originated as a result of the reducing of the pays of about sixty teachers and their resignations.

The students went on strike and demanded either the restoration of the pays of the teachers or proportionate cut in the salaries of both the lower and upper staff. The D. S. F. was approached for help and Mr. K. P. Shankara was deputed to look into the matter. Mr. Shankara with the help of the Old Boys' Association was able to bring about a compromise between the students and the Managing Committee. The students gained their point but the Federation incurred the displeasure of the Arabic College and school authorities, who refused the use of their premises for the functions of the Federation.

The second strike which continued for four months was the famous Tibbia College Strike. The immediate occasion of the strike was the dismissal of a professor on grounds of incompetency (which the authorities could not prove). But the real grievances at the root of the strike were the preferential treatment given by the authorities to *Unani*-section, forced study of anti-diluvian books, compulsory purchase of materials from the College stores, which sold things at much higher rate than the market The students also complained against the attitude of the Joint Secretary of the College. The strike continued for three months but the students' courage and persistency ultimately succeeded. The authorities rusticated the entire students of the *Ayurvedic*-section numbering about 200, and tried to divide the public and the students on communal grounds. They also shut the students in the hostel and closed their kitchens, and water, etc. This forced the D. S. F. to take the matter in its hands. The Sub-Committee of the D. S. F. through the press placed the whole situation before the public and sought its intervention. Consequently Mr. Asaf Ali M. L. A., Mr. Neki Ram Sharma, and others intervened; and after prolonged talks compromise was affected and the strike was called off.

Another strike which attracted the attention of the D. S. F. was the Khalsa College Strike led by Mr. Prabodh Chandra. The students of Delhi deputed Mr. K. P. Shankara, Meer Mushtaq Ahmad and Mr. Kanwar Lal to go to Amritsar to study the situation and report the same to the D. S. F. executive committee for further action. Fortunately the College authorities by the intervention of Baba Kharak Singh agreed to the demands of the students and hence the strike was called off.

CHAPTER XVII

STUDENT MOVEMENT IN OTHER PROVINCES

THE student movement in C. P., Behar, Kashmir and Sindh is of a recent growth and is yet in infancy. It would be quite appropriate to treat the movements there in one chapter.

CENTRAL PROVINCES

Student movement in C. P. is of a recent growth. Before 1934 there were nearly sixty organizations in the province, some working on national and others on the social basis.

In December 1935 at the time of the Golden Jubilee of the Indian National Congress the students of Nagpur organized themselves and shouldered the responsibility well by having a complete four days' programme of their own. Taking this very opportunity a Nagpur Students' Conference was held with Pandit Ravi Shankra Shukla in chair. The delegates numbered 577 and in this very conference it was decided to start a Nationalist Students' Association at Nagpur with an aim to organize the college and high school students by focussing their political aspirations and prepare them for taking due share in the struggle for complete national independence. This very organization sent a batch of sixteen delegates to the All-India Students' Conference at Lucknow—the highest number of delegates coming from outside U. P.

Just after the formation of the All-India Students' Conference branches of the All-India Students' Federation were established at Malkapur, Wardha, Jubbulpore and Amraoti.

BEHAR

There existed no student organization worth the name in Behar before the All-India Students' Federation came into existence. After its formation some workers from other provinces visited this province and exhorted students to organize themselves. Accordingly the Gaya District Students' Conference was held in April, 1937. This was followed by a series of conferences in other districts. All these conferences gave birth to many strong organizations which came into prominence just after these conferences.

The first April *hartal*, to protest against the imposition of the Government of India Act, 1935, without the consent and against the will of the people of India, was observed by the students all over Behar. Processions were taken out with slogans, "Down with the Slave Constitution". The police made *lathi*-charge and arrests. At Gaya young school children were publicly flogged by the police. During June, 1937, student organizations were formed at Gaya, Jehanabad, Patna and other cities.

The most important of the student organizations in the province is the Chhatra Sangh. Its activities are mainly directed towards students' moral, cultural and physical development. With these aims in view, a debating society and an athletic club have been organized. During the last six months six sittings were held and discussion took place on subjects like the widow remarriage, higher female education, caste-system, national education and vegetarian diet. This institution, under the inspiration of Babu Rajendra Prasad aims at serving the national cause and hence practical training is imparted under the supervision of talented teachers and veteran nationalist workers.

During the last elections to the Provincial Legislative Assembly, students worked hard in different constituencies for the Congress candidates.

KASHMIR

Mr. Prabodh Chandra of the Punjab Students' Federation paid a visit to Kashmir in June, 1937, in order to organize a powerful student movement in the Jammu and Kashmir

States. Though such a move was already afoot, yet the workers had some differences. The presence of Mr. Prabodh Chandra brought about a rapproachement between the two groups. He inaugurated the All-Kashmir Students' Federation and dissolved all unions and leagues that had loomed up among students. The Federation was affiliated to the Punjab Students' Federation.

In November, 1937, was held the 1st All-Kashmir Students' Conference under the presidentship of Dr. Ashraf. Its deliberations had a far-reaching effect upon the students. The student movement is gaining momentum day by day.

SINDH

The students of Sindh were called to the first consorted effort during the 1931 session of the Indian National Congress when the responsibility of holding the Second All-India Student Convention fell upon them. And they gave a proof of ample resourcefulness, when under the guidance of Sjt. Daulat Ram Jairam Das, Choeth Ram Gidwani and the leadership of Jai Singhani and Jethi Sepahi Milani (now a Congress M.L.A. to the Sindh Assembly) they made every arrangement for the success of this Convention. Since then the students have organized themselves at Karachi, Hyderabad and many other places. We shall be failing in our duty if we do not make a mention of Mr. Mohd. Amin Khoso (Congress M.L.A. to the Sindh Assembly) who was once a moving figure in the Aligarh University and who has revolutionized the student movement in Sindh. We are confident that under the lead of veteran student workers like Messrs. Khoso and Sepahi Milani, the student movement in Sindh would make a great headway.

Sindh Students' Conference.—In April, 1938, the Sindh students held their conference at Karachi. Sjt. Bhulabhai Desai, the leader of the opposition in the Central Assembly, who takes a keen interest in the student movement, presided over this Conference. He exhorted the students to unite themselves in the country's great fight for freedom. He wanted students to lend every support to the Sindh Ministry for ameliorating the condition of the masses.

CHAPTER XVIII

STUDENT MOVEMENT IN BURMA

THOUGH politically separate to-day, geographically and culturally Burma is a part and parcel of India. From its very inception the Burmese Student movement has been closely associated with the student movement in India.

The student movement in Burma began in 1920. The country was then in the midst of a great awakening and was on the eve of constitutional changes. The awakening was largely a reflection of political unrest in India. There was at that time in Burma a strong united political organization called "G. C. B. A."

It was at this time that the University of Rangoon Bill was introduced for the first University in Burma (it is still the only one). The Bill, from the outset, met with great opposition from the public because of its reactionary character. The government did not heed this public opinion and passed the Bill into the Act.

The result was a big strike of students of colleges and schools. Some government officers left their services and joined in the movement for national education which came as a sequel to the strike. A National College was founded, but did not last for long. National Schools were also founded throughout the country, and to-day about fifty of them have survived, partly through government aid. It must be said to the credit of these National Schools that they have played no small part in creating a national consciousness in the country. The day of the original strike was recognized as "National Day" in Burma by the ninth G. C. B. A. Conference held at Mandalay about 1923, as an indication of the sacrifice of the youth of the country for the cause of education and nationalism.

The University Act was slightly amended in 1924. By then there was already a split in the G. C. B. A. on the question of council entry, and from that time our country has been divided up into numerous factions and groups.

In 1923, when the economic crisis impinged itself on our country as on other parts of the world, there was again a revival of nationalism in a more intensive form. A strong move was made almost all over the country for consumption of national goods. Burmese commercial enterprises sprang up everywhere, though most of them died down again after a time.

As a result of the Simon Commission report the question of separation was raised, and the political changes to be made in Burma were widely discussed. The students, especially those in the University, were astir with enthusiasm, and were beginning to be more fully conscious of the conditions of the country. They took part in the "Buy Burmese" campaign, and an All-Burma Youth League was set up. The rebellion of the peasants in the Tharawaddy and some other districts was then at its height. An organization of young men known as "*Dobama Asiyone*," whose members are to-day called *Thakins*, sprang up. And these youth movements were largely sponsored by the more enthusiastic students of the University.

In the University itself, there was agitation against the high-handed actions of the University authorities. The Rangoon University Students' Union came into existence in January, 1931, and in the drafting of the constitution for this Union the students held their ground against the University authorities and succeeded in getting a constitution of their own making. From then onwards, the attitude of the University towards its students changed; and in its reports and in the educational reports issued at that period there were remarks about the students' being "perverted by political influence".

Affairs continued in this way, with ups and downs, till in February of last year a definite break came between the University and the students. The Union President was expelled from University College for a speech made on the occasion of the last Union meeting of the Session, which contained some remarks on the actions of the Principal of the College. The Editor of the Union Magazine, *Oway* ("Peacock"—the national bird of Burma) published a letter attacking certain members of the University. He was called to account for the bad language in which the letter was couched, and it was subsequently rumoured that he was to be expelled from the University.

Meanwhile, a mass meeting of the University students was called to consider the President's case. The result of the meeting was another big strike of the colleges and schools. This was on the 25th February, 1936. The strike ended on 10th May of the same year.

The All-Burma Students' Union, the first of its kind in Burma, was formed as a result of the first All-Burma Students' Conference held on the 8th and 9th May, 1936. By the formation of this Union, the students hoped to safeguard their rights and interests, to improve the educational system of Burma, to impart political education to the students and—above all—to bring together all the students of the country for community of thought, feeling and action for the greater struggle for freedom.

The students held the second All-Burma Students' Conference, at Mandalay (the old Burmese capital) on the 9th and 10th May.

It was attended by 400 student delegates from 27 towns, and three thousand people attended the opening session, which was addressed by Pandit Jawaharlal Nehru. We received several messages of good-will on this occasion from Europe, India and China.

Among other things, we have decided to affiliate the Union to the World Student Association. We have decided to publish our own journal in Burmese, to carry out a study of rural problems and the improvement of the conditions of the rural population, and to help in the establishment of the National University formed since last year. We have passed a resolution on anti-Imperialism, expressing a resolve not to take part in Imperialist wars. We will try to have the University of Rangoon Act amended during the year and agitate for more and better education.

The students of Burma have awakened, and what is more, have organized themselves! This fact is amply proved by the circular of the late officiating Director of Public Instructions in December last, which asked the Headmasters of the schools to use caution and discretion in regard to the growing Students' Unions which had been formed during the year.

No force, however great, can check the tide that is fast advancing. The Burmese students will march towards unity, towards greater understanding of world problems and conditions, and finally towards the freedom that is necessary, if the Burmese people are to co-operate fully with other nations for the cause of peace and civilization.

CHAPTER XIX

THE EDUCATED UNEMPLOYED IN INDIA

THE problem of the educated unemployed is the burning topic of the day in India as well as abroad. This problem in India is no more a sectional or provincial one. There is no single section of the educated youth in the country which is content with its lot. Graduates are being employed as police constables. Doctors of Philosophy with European qualifications are known to have applied for and failed in securing a job of an Assistant in the Registration Department or of Headmaster in a middle school. Suicides, crimes, lackeyism and instances of petty thefts and fraudulent deelings and of general demoralization are multiplying everyday. It appears as if the very life-blood of the Indian nation was being poisoned in the most delicate and vital part of body politic.

This is partly due to a peculiarity of the educated youth. Individualist to the core, the middle class young man refuses to recognize the social basis of his unemployment. As a typical petty bourgeois, he attributes his failures to his personal ill-luck and is always willing to cherish an illusion which helps in ensuring his egoism. This accounts for the general demoralization among the educated youth, created by a few and the prospectus which the Government employment offers to one in many thousands. Unless young men recognize the obvious fact that they suffer not as individuals but as a class and the cause of this suffering does not lie in accidental misfortune but in deep-laid and fundamental social evil, very little hope of solution can be held out to the educated and unemployed youth of India.

We are discussing the problem at a time when fortunately all that is important on the subject—facts, opinions, proposals, etc., have been formulated in a concrete shape. The central and the various provincial governments and Legislatures have expressed themselves on the problem; committees have investigated its various aspects and Commissions in other fields have already recorded their views on related aspects of the question. So that, more or less, we know exactly the nature of the problem to-day and what to expect from various quarters. As a matter of fact, of late, the reactions of any social demand have taken such a clear and patent lines of response that we can almost foretell in advance how particular classes will react to a given situation.

It is, therefore, only fair if we, on our part,

form some very clear opinions on certain aspects of the problem. It is very necessary to understand that in India the problem of educated unemployment directly arises from the contemporary position of British Imperialism in the world. With the establishment of British rule in India, from 1858 onwards, when the railways, roads, posts, telegraph and other modern methods of economic exploitation and political subjection were introduced and developed, a number of auxiliary services, technical cadres, and certain other professions necessarily came into existence; and to feed them a number of technical and educational institutions had to be provided. An indigenous industrial revolution would also have given birth to similar institutions but with the fundamental difference that in such economy, industrial and technical expansion and agricultural and educational developments would have balanced together. As it is, our educational and technical institutions have existed purely as an appendage to the Imperialist rule and it is only when the Imperialist requirements were met with, that the surplus of the educational and technical product began to look for an independent social basis in the country. It would not have been difficult to utilize this surplus if Imperialism was compatible with the economic expansion of a colonial nation under it. The slight industrial development that we see in

India is primarily a product of the peculiar conditions of the Great War. The other feudal classes of Indian princes and landlords which appear to be prosperous, are rather a drag on, than a help to our national economy.

It has been generally admitted that the problem of the unemployed to-day is not peculiar to any one country but is a world-problem. It did not exist in its present form before 1914. The problem does not exist in countries like Russia and Turkey even to-day. This means then that the problem of unemployment and growing impoverishment is necessarily connected with the predominant form of the world economy which prevails outside Russia or Turkey and which is undergoing a period of acute crisis on a world scale to-day. The world crisis of capitalism which set in 1929 nowhere shows any signs of abatement after nine years of attempts at capitalistic reconstruction. Curiously enough the present world crisis is a crisis of over production, of poverty in the midst of plenty.

It is important to realize that, as an integral part of the British Commonwealth, India is now linked up with the world market and is bound to be affected even more acutely from its reactions. After the Great War and the few years of boom that followed its wake, it was being generally felt that British Imperialism like the rest of the Capitalist world was again drifting towards an economic crisis even more complex than before. Mechanical and technical advances further pressed on the diminished resources of a shrunken world market. All this was a fatal blow to England, which is now no more the classic country of Free Trade and Liberalism. It is as much protectionist and dictatorial as any other. With the development of the world crisis the whole situation was precipitated in view of the impending danger of World War. The Disarmament Conference, the Economic Conference and the Naval and so many other conferences that were invited to solve the Capitalist and Imperialist contradictions on a world basis have utterly failed to register any improvement in the situation. As a result, the contemporary capitalist world is the vast military camp where alliances are being sought and armaments piled up for the inevitable conflict. Japan in China, Italy in Abyssinia and Germany in Austria have only made feeble beginning towards what is soon going to develop into a general engagement over a world front.

What does all this imply for us in India? It means that to meet this grave world crisis and this war situation, British Imperialism must exploit even more intensively than ever before the meagre resources of our country. It must be through every constitutional and administrative contrivance. The Indian market and Indian men and money are more in demand to-day than ever before to save the threatened Empire. The central problem of every present-day Imperialist country is exploitation and yet more intensive exploitation of colonial lands.

The educated middle class in India finds itself in a very anomalous and embarrassing situation to-day. Generally speaking, the educated youth do not find the same scope as before in the Government services or in any of the professions of law, medicine, engineering, trade, commerce or agriculture and industry. We, the educated unemployed, look to the Government for help ; the Government in its turn looks to the world market and trade conditions, and the world market looks upto the next World War to save it! Hence we find in our country a growing defence and military budget. Unless we try to overthrow the whole system of capitalist and Imperialist economy we do not see how we can rationally expect to get anything out of British Imperialism to-day.

Of late, wave of acute mass poverty has spread all over India. Knowing as we do something of the psychology of our administrators and their outlook on Indian social problems, it would not have been very much mattered to them if the problem of unemployment was confined to the inarticulate masses of the country. But once it began to affect the educated young men, the whole problem assumed a different administrative aspect for these youth were vocal and could be politically dangerous. Not that the imperialist could do anything to relieve that greater unemployment among the masses; but it just pretended to be doing something, just to keep these youth in expectancy and away from mischief.

The insoluble contradiction is somewhat as follows: Government must permit the industrialization of the country on a big scale or as an alternative divert huge funds to maintain them. But Imperialism is incompatible with the industrial expansion of a colonial country and has already drained the country of the wealth which could be employed in these schemes of social betterment. Hence every serious attempt at the solution of a social problem, to begin with, resolves itself into a political programme for a radical transference of political and economic power from the British Imperialist to the Indians.

As early as 1926 the question of middle-class unemployment came up for discussion before the Central Legislature. When the Government of India was pressed for investigation, it passed it on to the provincial governments. At the Universities Conference held at Delhi in 1934, H. E. Lord Willingdon, the Viceroy, speaking on the problem of the educated unemployed observed that "unmerited disappointments accentuated by irksome inactivity, are apt to lead high-spirited young men to dangerous and unexpected channels. I am well aware that Universities cannot by themselves create development in industry and commerce. In this respect they are enchained to forces over which they have really no control; but it is undoubtedly within the province of the educational authorities to so adjust the general scheme of education that the bent of students and pupils shall be turned towards occupations best suited to them." The Educational Commission to the Government of India has not been slow in popularizing the same policy. In this case the Government of India are following a consistent policy which amounts to this: We do not want any longer all these Universities for our requirements; we are unwilling to permit any great industrialization or economic expansion; hence the Universities and higher education in general must go, particularly now as it is producing in the country a politically conscious and hence an undesirable element.

We have tried to analyse the situation with a view to bring out the two cardinal facts, *viz.*, (1) that educated unemployment directly arises from the course of the world development of capitalism and the political and economic dependence of India on Great Britain; (2) that all solutions which do not realize this fundamental proposition are unreal and utterly inadequate to meet the demands of our solution.

CHAPTER XX

STUDENTS AND POLITICS

INDIA at present is a peculiar country and the questions that are raised surprise one. Some even argue that the independence of India is bad for India ; that something less than independence is really more than it. We find some difficulty in understanding these abstruse problems. Yet another peculiar question relates to students and politics. 'Students in India must not take part in politics,' some say. What is politics? According to the usual interpretation in India (official India), to assist or support the Government in any way is not politics ; but to criticize or work against the existing order in India is politics.

Quite a senior students in India possess a vote for provincial legislatures. To vote is to take part in politics ; to vote intelligently necessitates the understanding of political issues ; to understand political issues results usually in accepting a certain political policy ; and if a student accepts that policy, as a citizen it is his duty to push forward that policy, to try to convert others to it. Thus inevitably a voter must be a politician ; and he should be an ardent politician if he is a keen citizen. Only those who lack political or social sense can remain passive and neutral or indifferent.

Even apart from his duty as a voter, every student must, if he is properly trained, prepare himself for life and its problems. Otherwise his education has been a waisted effort. Politics and economics deal with these problems and no person is properly educated unless he understands them. Perhaps it is difficult for most people to see a clear path through life's jungle. But whether we know the solution of the problem or not, we must at least know the nature of it. What are the questions that life puts to us? The answer may be difficult; but the curious thing is that people seek to answer without knowing the real question. No serious or thoughtful student can take up this futile attitude.

The various 'isms that play such an important part in world to-day—nationalism, liberalism, socialism, communism, imperialism, fascism, etc., are efforts on the part of various groups to answer these questions. Which answer is correct? Or are they all steeped in error? In any event we have to choose. We must know and have capacity to choose correctly. This cannot be done if there are repressions and suppressions of thought and action. It cannot be done properly if High Authority sits on us and prevents the free play of the mind.

WORKERS OF THE KASHMIR STUDENTS' FEDERATION

Janki Nath Zutshi

Kashi Nath Kaul

WORKERS OF THE KASHMIR STUDENTS' FEDERATION

G. M. D. Hamdani, President
All-Kashmir Students' Federation, 1937-38

K. N. Bamzai, President, Sirinagar Students' Union

Thus it becomes necessary for all thinking individuals, and more so for the students than for others, to take the fullest theoretical part in politics. Naturally this will apply to the senior students at life's threshold rather than the junior students who are still far from these problems. But a theoretical consideration is not enough for a proper understanding; even theory requires practice. From the point of view of study alone students must leave their lecture halls and investigate reality in village and town, in field and factory, to take part to some extent in the various activities of the people, including political activities.

One has ordinarily to draw the line somewhere. A student's first business is to train his mind and body and make them instruments of thought, understanding and action. Before he is trained he cannot think or act effectively. Yet the training comes not from listening to pious advice, but by indulging in action to some extent. That action under normal conditions, must be subordinated to theoretical training. But it cannot be eliminated or else the training itself is deficient.

It is our misfortune that in India our educational system is thoroughly lop-sided. But an even greater misfortune is the highly authoritarian atmosphere that surrounds it. Not in education alone, but everywhere in India, red-liveried, pompous and often empty-headed authority seeks to mould people after its own pattern and prevent the growth of the mind and the spread of ideas. Recently we saw how this authority made a mess of things even in the realm of sports. In our Universities this spirit of authority reigns supreme and, in the name of discipline, comes down heavily on any one who does not meekly obey. They do not like the qualities that are encouraged in free countries, the spirit of daring, the adventures of the soul in uncharted regions. It is not surprizing then that we do not produce many men and women who seek to conquer the Poles or Everest, to control the elements and bring them to man's use, to hurl defiance at man's ignorance and timidity and inertia and littleness and try to raise him upto the stars.

Must students take part in politics? Must they take part in life, a full wholesome part in life's varied activities, or be of the clerkly breed, carrying out orders from above? As students they cannot keep out of politics, as Indian students even more so they must keep touch with them. Yet it is true that normally the training of their minds and bodies must be their principal consideration during this period of their growth. They must observe a certain discipline but that discipline should not be such as crushes the mind and kills the spirit.

So, normally. But abnormal conditions

come when normal rules are swept away. During the Great War where were the students of England, France and Germany? Not in their Colleges but in the trenches, facing and meeting death. Where are the students of Spain and China to-day.

A subject country is always to some extent in an abnormal condition. So is India to-day. And in considering these problems, we must also consider our environments and the growing abnormality in the world. And as we seek to understand it, we are driven to take part, however little it might be, in the chapter of events.

CHAPTER XXI

STUDENT STRIKES IN INDIA

STUDENT strikes are a very important part of the student movement in India. These strikes are very common and for the last few years, these strikes have gained in number. We need not go into the local grievances, and the causes of particular strikes at particular places. We must understand their psychology in order to understand them. For the past few years we have been witnessing a growing unrest in the student community in its various ebbs and tides. Whenever the whole country is infected with some predominant idea, the students as its constituent part also find themslves in abnormal circumstances. Then the usual repressive regime comes in the wake. The government does everything for the 'peace, tranquility and good government of India'. People are put behind the bars, press is gagged and so on and so forth. The students share their lot in such ordeals. But the matters do not end there. Students have to face yet another 'keeper of tranquility and order'—the educational authorities which are bureaucratic and narrow in their outlook. There are fines, rustications, expulsions and public-caning to maintain discipline with an iron-hand.

Further, the students of India have been intellectually bankrupt. The Maculian system of education does not equip them for the arena of life. The students know that after their educational career they have to throw their lot with the common folk, who cannot make both ends meet, despite working from morn till night. Sometimes they get an opportunity to listen to their leaders who have at least soothing words for them and promise a haven of panacea for the 'good time coming'. Moreover, a student is a being of flesh and blood, his routine is not merely to sit in the class-room and pour over the barren leaves. Being a citizen he is never immune from the influence of external circumstances. He sees the naked treading in the street, he heaves a sigh for them. He feels that India is under a foreign yoke, he sheds a tear in slavery. In short, the narrow outlook of the educational authorities and the force of circumstances lead student to strike.

These innumerable student strikes are not liked by our national leaders. They are of opinion that these strikes lead to indiscipline. We on our part would never support any strike which leads to any indiscipline. In fact, discipline is an essential ingredient of our national life. Unfortunately, these leaders do not care to know and examine the various causes which lead to these strikes. Let us assure them that students resort to strikes only when they have tried all other avenues for rectifying their grievances; only when they find their self-respect at stake ; only when the educational authorities want to shut out any progressive ideology among them. Let us enumerate some of the causes that lead to strikes at various places. The Khalsa College, Amritsar strike started when the college authorities wanted to penalize the nationalist professors and with that end in view were carrying on sinister propaganda against them. The students of the Lahore Ayurvedic College resorted to strike, when their principal in his authoritativeness punished students, imposed heavy fines and expelled some of them. The Fyzabad (U. P.) students left their classes when some of the students who went to hear Mrs. Sarojini Naidu were fined. The Cawnpore D.A.-V. College students protested to attend classes when their principal issued a *ukasa* f or not taking part in the last Provincial assembly elections. The Tibbia College (Dehli) students went on strike when they began to receive a step-motherly treatment from the college-authorities and when they were ordered to buy every thing from the college stores which charged very high prices.

Gandhiji is of opinion that the question of student strikes should not arise at all in the Congress provinces, as if the very presence of the Congress ministers would solve all student problems. Gandhiji does not appreciate that students have some local grievance, too; they are to be amicably settled between the teacher and the taught and thus require no outside interference.

Those who condemn student strikes do not care to keep in view the basis on which a strong movement like that of the students can be built, grown and strengthened. The students can only be rallied under the banner of their common grievances. Political problems are not so fascinating to them. Appreciation of local problems, their understanding in true perspective and strikes are the essential ingredients for the growth of a radical student movement. Bereft of these, it is likely to be engulfed in a quagmire of vagueness.

We again emphasize that student strikes generally have little political tinge and they are cry against an encroachment upon student-rights. If at all students have to resort to a strike, they do so not in a hostile manner; but just to defend their rights and to organize themselves on a wider and stronger basis. If our leaders want that students of India must learn to respect and defend their rights, they would surely eulogize such student-strikes.

Below we give an account of a few student

strikes, in order to mobilize public opinion in their favour; and in order to understand the psychology behind them.

Bombay Matric Results Strike.—In June 1936, the students of Bombay Presidency cast of their lethargy and lassitude when the shocking Matric Results were out and the martial spirit once again visible in the rank and file promised the return of historic days of 1928. The Bombay Students' Brotherhood was the first in the field to champion the cause of the victims of the 'Matric Massacre'. Under its auspices meetings, processions and *hartals* were organized to condemn the action of the University Czars in reducing the Matric results to the shocking percentage of 28. When the constitutional means were denied to the students, they decided to march in procession to the Senate Hall to present their grievances. The senators did not condescend to see the student-representatives. On the contrary, some of them were frightened out of their wits and rang for a *posse* of the *lathi* police. The lawyer-leader comrade S. Batliwala presented the students' case before the University lords so logically and eloquently that the latter despite their resentment at the unceremonious entrance into the hall, were spell-bound till he finished his speech. The strike terminated after a fortnight when some of the senators promised to reconsider the matter.

Aligarh Strike.—In October, 1936 certain students of the Muslim University were expelled for some alleged misbehavior. In fact, these students attracted the attention of the University authorities by rousing a national spirit amongst the students and the authorities expelled them under this pretext. The students could not sacrifice their progressive colleagues so very easily and so they went on a strike, which compelled the authorities to close down the institution for the *Dussehra* holidays before time. The students stayed on, although the authorities closed the hostels and the kitchens. The authorities paid the railway fare to some students to send them away. On the re-opening of the University the authorities had to take back the expelled students before peace was restored in the University.

The Khalsa College Strike.—This strike was perhaps unique in the history of the student movement in India. It took place in June, 1937 and lasted for as many as twenty days. Above all it was crowned with a magnificent success. It attracted the attention of almost all the student organizations in India and student workers from Aligarh, Lucknow, Cawnpore, Delhi, Kapurthala, Moga, Rawalpindi and Lahore actually took part in making this strike a success.

This strike originated when the Principal of the college refused to the request of a deputation of students who waited upon him, to stop the circulation of an indecent pamphlet issued against Professor Niranjan Singh, a nationalist and a most popular teacher in the province. The Principal did not agree, also, to publicly condemn this tract. The students very peacefully conveyed to the Principal that they would not attend their classes as a protest against the publication of that sinister tract. The Principal lost his balance of mind and in indignation rusticated those students. The sutdents could not tolerate this intrusion upon their civil rights and self-respect.

The Principal now acted with the least imprudence. He summoned the police and many students including the President of the Provincial Students' Union, Secretary Provincial Students' Union, and Secretary, Lahore Students' Union were made a target of a severe *lathi*-charge. This incident elicited sympathy from all sections of the people in the province and abroad. Now the students decided to continue their strike till the rusticated students were taken back, the Principal expressed regret for his behavior and openly condemned the *lathi*-charge. The college authorities acted most foolishly. They patted the Principal and endorsed his action. It appeared that the whole of the 'drama' was preconceived by the persons at the helm of affairs.

It was really painful to see hundreds of students lying prostrate on the ground before the college gate, the ladies singing '*utho naujawano badal do zamana'* (arise ye youngmen and change the times) and many leaders and spectators watching everything with keen interest. Yet more painful was the sight to see the Principal with some 'loyal professors' at the gate—the guardian of students who lay prostrate in the scorching sunshine before him! Still he had the cheek to come out every morning with a statement that many students attended the classes!

After full two weeks the strikers changed their tactics. They broke the 'monotony' of picketing when Mr. Prabodh Chandra announced, that in order to assert their rights to enter the college premises, he would lead a *jatha*. The police was summoned. As soon as this *jatha* got in, it was put under arrest. Then was led the second *jatha*; but the magistrate at the spot acted very tactfully. He let the first *jatha* too and declared that none was placed under arrest. This gave the strikers a moral victory. But the Principal was still blind to all these happenings. Believing in the false notions of prestige and not caring for the interests of the institution and his students, he 'promulgated' that forty ring-leaders of the strike were also rusticated.

Baba Kharak Singh now appeared on the scene. He wanted to settle everything amicably. The students placed their demands before Babaji and appointed him as their sole arbitrator. He carried on the negotiations. The demands of the students were acceded to and all the rusticated students were taken back.

The Lucknow Christian College Strike.—This strike of the Lucknow students, in October, 1937 was the spontaneous outburst of a past troublous system of heavy fines in the Athletic Department, which swelled to more than Rs. 600 a month. The Athletic Director was approached, but he turned out the students from his office. The students could not tolerate this high-handedness. The next day they went on strike. The students of the college under the guidance of the Lucknow Students' Federation formed a strike committee with Mr. Mohd. Khurshed as its president. This committee put forward the demands before the Principal. The negotiations between the authorities and the students continued for full five days and the strike continued side by side. The most remarkable feature of the strike was that not even a single student attended the college and there was no picketing at the college gates. On the second day the students of the Christian School, yet another institution under the same management, joined the strikers. Their demands were the same.

The result of this five-day complete strike was that the authorities conceded to all the demands ton the sixth day of the strike.

The Lahore Ayurvedic College Strike.—This strike took place in September, 1937 and continued till April, 1938. Serious trouble had brewed in the Dayanand Ayurvedic College. The students of this institution since quite a long time had many just grievances against the Principal. In addition to being utterly incapable in teaching, he had been in the habit of levying heavy fines on the slightest provocation, and his behaviour towards the students and staff had been objectionable. All these grievances were placed by the students before the managing committee of the college, but the managing committee did not take any notice of these. So the students had to resort to a general strike which continued for about six months. Not a single student attended the classes; and several members of the staff also sent in their resignations. The Lahore Students' Union intervened and the strike terminated successfully. The managing committee cancelled orders of rustication against the strikers and promised to take away all the teaching work and executive powers from the Principal. In fact, these promises of the managing committee were not given effect at all. During the Xmas of 1937 the authorities closed the college for three months, without caring for their promises or the interests of the students.

The college was to re-open on the 1st of April, 1938. Picketing was resorted to by the students on the night of the 31st March and it continued day and night. Not a single student attended the classes. The authorities approached the local dailies, which totally refused to give publicity to the students' case. The students wanted to migrate to other institutions; but the authorities of these institutions being in league with the college authorities showed their unwillingness to admit the students. The students had to fight this battle single-handed and on the righteousness of their demands. The Lahore Students' Union now came on the scene. The President of the Punjab Students' Federation and the General Secretary of the Lahore Students' Union, while exhorting the students to stand solidly and peacefully by their demands, were arrested along with forty other students on a complaint of rioting lodged by the Principal. Now some local leaders began to carry on the negotiations with the managing committee after nearly twenty days of the strike. Better counsels prevailed. The college authorities took back all the rusticated students and also withdrew all the teaching and executive powers from the Principal. He had nothing to do with the students. Thus this strike terminated successfully after about six months.

CHAPTER XXII

INTERNATIONAL STUDENT MOVEMENT AND INDIA

UNDER the leadership of Pandit Jawaharlal Nehru the whole of India became international-minded after 1934. The resolutions of the Indian National Congress and the news papers have begun to recognize the force of international events and give them due publicity.

The All-India Students' Federation from its very inception had this sense of appreciation for international problems. Moreover, the inaugural address of Pandit Jawaharlal Nehru at the Lucknow Conference called upon the students to understand these problems which affect India vitally. He said, " I will talk for a while about various big questions which do not perhaps immediately affect you, but which, I think have a vital consequence for each one of us. Now tell me, what do you think has the question of Palestine to do with the students in India ? Most of them do not know about it except as something entirely separate and different from their daily life and activities. For the matter of that this question and the great tragedy that is taking place in Spain to-day, what has that to do with the students in India? Has that any consequence? I may tell you that the question of Spain, Europe and of Palestine has far greater interest for me than all the odd news that newspapers tell me. Why, I will tell. Not because I attach less importance to matters which concern India immediately, but because these happenings affect you and India and the whole of the world." The 1st All-India Students' Conference amongst other resolutions, passed a resolution condemning the Imperialist wars laying: "This Conference views with great apprehension the menancing advance of such forces of cultural destrucion as the Imperialist Wars; and calls upon the student world to resist these forces and not to participate in any such war".

Just after the Lucknow session the All-India Students' Federation, carried on correspondence and established connections with the World Student Association, Paris and the International Student Service, Geneva. These two international student organizations gave a wide publicity to the All-India Students' Federation. So much so that queries poured in from England, America and China.

The 2nd All-India Students' Conference at Lahore discussed many international student problems. It passed the following resolutions to

AMRITSAR AND KAPURTHALA STRIKERS

STRIKERS

OF

THE KHALSA COLLEGE, AMRITSAR

Dewan Chaman Lal addressing the strikers

Procession of the strikers

condemn the fascist insurgents in Spain: "This Conference condemns the fascist insurgents who have risen against the lawful and established Spanish Government and places on record its heartfelt sympathy for the students of Spain who are fighting bravely for defending the freedom of their nation." This Conference also decided to affiliate the All-India Students' Federation with the World Student Association, Paris; in view of the fact that one of the objects of the All-India Students' Federation is to encourage intellectual co-operation between Indian students and students abroad. Thus it was in November, 1936 that the Student Movement In India was linked with the international student movement.

Mention may also be made of the *Students' Tribune*—the official organ of the All-India Students' Federation—which has been doing the greatest service of broadcasting international problems among the students and creating an appreciation for the same. This journal has been giving the widest publicity to the doings of the World Student Association and the International Student Service. Regular reports from James Klugmann, Secretary World Student Association, Paris have become a common feature of this journal. Apart from this, articles on International War, Help Spanish Democracy, Principles of Education in Soviet Russia and many other international student topics are regularly published in this journal.

The All-India Students' Federation has also been doing its utmost to create an appreciation for the current world problems. It called upon various student organizations to observe Spain Day, China-Day, Anti-War Day and Student-Day. The Lahore Students Union in May, 1936 celebrated the Spain Week. Lectures were delivered on the history and the prevailing forces in Spain. A small tract containing the history of Spain and an appeal for funds to protect the Spanish democracy was published. The sale-proceeds of this booklet were sent to Spain.

The China-Day in August, 1936 was observed with due eclat throughout India. Students all over India passed resolutions for the boycott of Japanese goods. The Bombay students took out processions carrying placards and raising slogans against the Japanese aggression. They also arranged an exhibition where they displayed porters of the Fascist War in China.

The Madras Students Organization in February, 1937 observed the Anti-War Day. They published a tract named *Why Anti-War Day* in which they traced the history of the world politics and then atural conflict of the Imperialist and Socialistic tendencies.

The various branches of the All-India Students' Federation gave full publicity to the proceedings of the World Student Conference

(1936), Paris. The Indian students felt much jubilated when Indian students overseas met at London on January 8, 1937. This meeting was called on the initiative of the Oxford and Cambridge Majlis; and representatives present were of the Indian Student Associations of about ten English Universities, London, Oxford, Cambridge, Manchester, Newcastle, together with fraternal delegates from the English Universities. This meeting formed 'Federation of Indian Students' Societies in Great Britain and Ireland' and expressed its solidarity with the All-India Students' Federation.

During July and August 1937 Mr. Kumarmandlam, Secretary of the Federation of Indian Student Societies, London, paid us a visit. He observed very keenly the activities of the All-India Students' Federation and acquainted us with the international student movement. He delivered lectures at many important places.

In April 1938 came that amiable personality, Mr. James Klugmann, secretary, World Student Association, Paris to India along with an International Students' Delegation to China. His presence, though for a fortnight, was fully utilized. He went to almost all the important educational centres in India. He was much impressed by the strong and wide-spread student movemement in India. He remarked, "The All-India Students' Federation is the greatest organization in the world; and the student movement in India is strongest amongst all the colonial student movements."

The All-India Students' Federation took yet another step to establish a stronger link with the international student movement. In January, 1938, the All-India Students' Federation elected Mr. Prabodh Chandra of the Punjab Students' Federation as its sole delegate to the World Student Conference, Budapest (Hungry) and the World Youth Conference, New York (U.S.A.). We are confident that the impending visit of Mr. Prabodh Chandra to these international conferences would prove much beneficial to our movement ând would cement our relations with the international student movement.

CHAPTER XXIII

TENDENCIES IN THE STUDENT MOVEMENT

HAVING known the activities of the All-India Students' Federation and its various branches, let us analyse the various tendencies prevailing in the student movement. During 1919-1923 there were abnormal times in India. The 'Congress' had launched a Non-Co-operation movement for the repeal of repressive laws and constitutional advancement. There were *hartals*, processions and protest meetings everywhere. The Indian students were not immune from these repercussions. Sense of patriotism appealed to them. They left schools and colleges and courted imprisonment. This was merely a stage of sentimentalism. Without reasoning the utility or implication of their activities, without understanding the meanings of 'Swaraj' and 'Satyagrah,' they joined this Civil Disobedience movement. So there was no visible tendency except that of patriotism.

From 1927 to 1929 there were some subversive violent activities in the Punjab and Bengal. Moreover some youth movements came into existence, namely Naujwan Bharat Sabha in the Punjab, Tarun Sangh in U. P. and Youth League in Bombay. These organizations with their radical programme, had a great fascination for the young. And as every adolescent has a liking for something new and sentimental, so some students joined the revolutionary parties. Some of them figured as accused in the conspiracy cases. But it must be remembered that these young men never advocated violent revolution from the student platforms. Whenever they joined any party,' they resigned from the student organizations. We need not enter into a discussion on these activities. From these activities one thing becomes quite clear. Indian students during the course of time developed a great hatred against the British rule. This explains why there were attempts upon the lives of some English and Indian officers, who were instrumental for perpetuating the regime of slavery and repression.

During 1930-32 the Congress launched another Civil Disobedience movement. This movement penetrated into remote villages. The Indian students played their due share in this movement too. They courted imprisonment. A number of the student organizations were declared unlawful. The students came out wiser through this ordeal. The faculty of reasoning developed in them and they paused to think what 'Swaraj' and Satyagrah' really mean. They began to look with a great doubt if the Gandhian Satyagrah could win them their ultimate objective. They felt that the success of their fight depended upon the support of the masses and the sympathy of foreign nations. The dynamic personality of Pandit Jawaharlal played a great part to bring about this change in outlook and appreciation for international problems.

This brings us to the present times. Under the new Act the Congress has assumed power in seven out of eleven provinces. There is some freedom of discussion and speech. Looking to the present conditions, we find various tendencies among the students.

In the first instance, there are students who think of joining some government or imperial services. They do not interest themselves in any activities. They hate a 'turbulent' life. They are shut to any ideology whatsoever. But these are a few in number; and they belong to the upper middle class.

Then there are students who want to organise student movement on the every-day demands of the students, *viz.* change in the system of education, reduction in fees, better system for examinations, etc. They want that students should not be swayed by the outside political influence. They want that student organizations should neither discuss nor take any active or passive part in any political programme.

They have some justification for their attitude. They are of opinion that during academical career, they cannot afford to indulge in activities which do not fall within their purview.

There are other students (and in an overwhelming majority) who think that student organizations must identify themselves with the programme of the Congress and students must take a due share in the fight for national emancipation. This section of students is most popular among students and public.

Then there is a progressive class of students. It clearly understands and appreciates the necessity of class consciousness. These students want to organize the students on the trade union bases without any influence from any political party. They want to unite students for 'knowing and defending their rights'. This class wants the students to study the vital problems of the day, enter into academical discussions on them, and if need be to do their best to bring a class consciousness amidst the lower class ranks. They are in no way hostile to the Congress programme. They are ready to form any united front with the Congress on any problem of common concern. This class has a firm conviction that it is only the lower-middle or the proletariat class—the farmers and the labourers in India—which would form a vangaurd in the fight for liberation of India. They know that the upper middle class cannot go a long way and sacrifice its vested interests at the altar of national freedom. On the other hand, the teeming masses have no vested interests whatsoever; they have nothing to lose but their chains.

This ideology is welcome on the grounds that it has a scientific perspective in its background. Considering the political, economic and international conditions, this tendency appears to be the only correct one. Otherwise there appears no solution for the growing unemployment in face of the rapid and irregular increase in the population of India.

This tendency is gaining ground; and the spontaneous student strikes, processions and protest meetings for defending their rights and in sympathy with Abyssinia, Spain and China, protesting against the agression of imperialist nations, speaks in clear and unequivocal terms that this tendency is to dominate and to play an important role in future.

CHAPTER XXIV

CONCLUSION

DURING a short span of two years the student movement in India has progressed with rapid strides. The organizational stage, which usually takes years, has been surpassed within this short-period. We find the branches of the All-India Students' Federation throughout the length and breadth of the country. Its membership also has run into many thousands.

The All-India Students' Federation is confronted yet with more important and serious problems. It must develop into a mass organization because it is to bring together students of every colour, shade or opinion. Of late, some student workers are of opinion that the Federation must propagate progrssive ideology. We are in complete agreement with them. But at the same time we must point out the danger attendant with it. Sometimes in our zeal we bring in those activities to the students' domain which would be the concern of some trade union or political party. It is this tactlessness that must be avoided. We must not arouse any suspicion in the minds of students that we are playing a second fiddle to any political party. For that the All-India Students' Federation should publish a thesis supplementing its constitution.

Keeping its individuality, the Federation must identify with the popular movements in the country. It is then and then only that it will live, become vigorous and attract larger number of students. It is quite pleasing to note that students of Ċ. P. have volunteered themselves to join the Vidya Mandir scheme, which is an experiment of the Wardha Educational Scheme. The Bombay students too are attending classes to equip themselves fully for launching a campaign against illiteracy in the presidency. The U. P. Rural Uplift Department is training more than forty students in various agricultural colleges for carrying on the rural uplift work. All these activities will go a long way to build the student movement on a stronger and lasting basis.

Student strikes in India have grown in number during the past year. Some of our lerders do not look upon them with an eye of approval. The All-India Students' Federation must define its attitude towards them. It must clarify how far these strikes are justified.

We fully hope that the Federation would take stock of all these things and carry on its activities in a very clear and all-embracing perspective.

APPENDIX I

CHARTER OF STUDENT-RIGHTS AS ADOPTED BY THE A.I.S.F. AT ITS LAHORE SESSION

(This charter contains governing principles according to which special rights and demands in each particular part of the country may be formulated.)

WHEREAS the student of to-day is the citizen of tomorrow.

Whereas under the peculiar condition of the country, the student is sought to be suppressed, his desire to know and learn confined to the four corners of text-books, his ability to develop his individual talent consistent with the advancement of his country materially checked, his potentiality in the cause of freedom consciously marred ;

Whereas the State or the Community, the Educational Authorities, the Parents and Guardians, the tripe authorities with which the student has to deal, have mainly neglected, or been indifferent to the rights of students ;

We declare that it is the fundamental and inalienable rights of the Indian students to claim :

I. The right to serve the country in all forms and directions consistent with its interests ;

II. The right to receive education free from cold-blooded utilitarianism or orthodoxy, so as to be equipped with adequate knowledge of general scientific principles underlying the chief productive activities of the modern age, as well as to develop the qualities of intellectual alertness, initiative, inventiveness, habit of rational thought, and a firm and disciplined character;

III. The right to secure abolition of education which is anti-national in tone or substance, which is sectarian or perpetuates class distinction or intensifies class divergence;

IV. The right to cultivate the living sense of national solidarity and social progress and to that end not being considered private property or exclusive concern of Parents or Guardians or teachers of a particular educational institution;

V. The right to secure development of the inherent facilities of each student, with a view to unfold his natural bent or aptitude, consistent with the needs of the country;

VI. The right to obtain untainted education and training free or at minimum cost and without legal or social impediment, so that illiteracy be wiped out from the country:

VII. The right to a greater proportion of public revenue for making education cheap and preferably free;

VIII. The right to be provided with educational institutions which are not run on profit-making principles of commercialism;

IX. The right to be provided with qualified teachers who have an aptitude for teaching; the teaching profession being provided with a living wage, insurance against accident, sickness or death, facilities for being up-to-date in their subject and pedagogic theory and experiments as courses of studies combining theory with practice, connecting abstract science with applied science, linking class-room studies with active life around, fostering national culture, national history and national language ;

XI. The right to freedom of thought, speech and association, in and outside the educational institutions, as an indispensable essential of civilised life.

XII. The right of recognition of Student Unions in all matters affecting the education and well-being of the Student Community ;

XIII. The right to be associated with the internal administration of educational institutions, and to a measure of Self-Government so far as the regulation of the conduct and morals of the students are concerned.

XIV. The right to get books, instruments and apparatus necessary for the spread of knowledge free of Government tax or private profit ;

XV. The right to be provided with adequate reading rooms, libraries, play-grounds, recreation facilities, cultural and health centres, the radio, cinema and press in and around schools and colleges ;

XVI. The right to be freed from the bogey of examinations, and till such time as they are abolished, to receive fair treatment in examinations securing facility to display all the knowledge the student may have acquired, as also any special talent or inherent excellence he may possess, with the provision for appeal to a competent authority in case of unjust treatment or unduly severe test ;

XVII. The right to be governed by a scientific code of permissible punishments, providing for well as complete freedom of thought and action in educational matters ;

X. The right to receive education imparted with the aid of well-balanced curricula, and necessary discipline, for efficient studies and banning all punishments (*e.g.*, whipping, beating, fining, expelling, etc.), inconsistent with human dignity and self-respect of the student ;

XVIII. The right to be safe-guarded against the stigma of inferiority cast by foreign Universities and to be provided with facilities to join institutions of different regions, Indian or foreign, on a footing of equivalence, without the stand of inferiority or partial treatment ;

XIX. The right of Employment, once the necessary minimum of prescribed knowledge and training is received by the student, thus guaranteeing opportunity for using this knowledge and training in order to contribute to the aggregate wealth of the country ;

XX. The right to be helped in the achievement of the above rights by organizations of parents, teachers and educationists in general.

APPENDIX II

OFFICE-BEARERS

OF THE

ALL-INDIA STUDENTS' FEDERATION

(Affiliated to the World Students Association)

1938-39

Central Office:

LITERATURE PALACE LUCKNOW.

General Secretary:

Ansar Harvani	(Aligarh)

Joint Secretaries:

Yagyadatt Sharma	(Delhi)
Lalitashankar	(C.P.)
Anant Patnaik	(Orissa)
M. B. Punaih	(Andhra)
Vacant	(Mysore)

Members of the Working Committee:

Miss Shanta Gandhi	(Bombay)
Prabodh Chandra	(Punjab)
Bhagwant Rai	(Punjab)
M. L. Shah	(Bombay)
Prem Narayan Bhargava	(U. P.)
M. A. Hamid Beg	(Madras)
Y. R. K. Prasad	(Madras)
Baidyanath Rath	(Orissa)
Dinesh Chowdhury	(Assam)
Ismail Madha	(Delhi)
Amirchand	(Punjab)
Pramode Sen	(Bengal)
Bishwanath Mukerjee	(Bengal)
R. K. Gupta	(U. P.)
Deonandan Sahai	(C. P.)
Bishwanath Dube	(Bengal)

PROMINENT WORKERS

OF

THE JULLUNDUR STUDENTS' UNION

D. P. Mohindra

Darshan Lal

Yogeshwar Sanyal

Ayudhia Prakash Pathik

PROMINENT WORKERS

OF

THE MOGA STUDENTS' UNION

Baldev Singh Randhawa, President

Jagwant Rai

Tirath Ram, Genl.-Secy.